BENT IRON WORK

BENT IRON WORK

(INCLUDING ELEMENTARY ART METAL WORK)

WITH NUMEROUS ENGRAVINGS AND DIAGRAMS

EDITED BY

PAUL N. HASLUCK

EDITOR OF " WORK " AND " BUILDING WORLD,"
AUTHOR OF " HANDYBOOKS FOR HANDICRAFTS," ETC. ETC.

PHILADELPHIA

DAVID McKAY, Publisher

1022, *MARKET STREET*

1903

Bent Iron Work

by Paul N. Hasluck

Originally published by
David McKay, Publisher
Philadelphia
1903

Reprinted by
Lindsay Publications Inc
Bradley IL 60915

ISBN 1-55918-184-2

1 2 3 4 5 6 7 8 9 0

1996

PREFACE.

THIS Handbook contains, in a form convenient for everyday use, a comprehensive digest of the knowledge of bent iron work and elementary art metal work, scattered over about twenty thousand columns of WORK— one of the weekly journals it is my fortune to edit —and supplies concise information on the details of the subjects on which it treats.

In preparing for publication in book form the mass of relevant matter contained in the volumes of WORK, much had to be arranged anew, altered, and largely re-written. From these causes the contributions of many are so blended that the writings of individuals cannot be distinguished for acknowledgment.

Readers who may desire additional information respecting special details of the matters dealt with in this Handbook, or instructions on kindred subjects, should address a question to WORK, so that it may be answered in the columns of that journal.

P. N. HASLUCK.

La Belle Sauvage, London.
December, 1902.

CONTENTS.

CHAP.   PAGE

   I.—Tools and Materials 9

  II.—Bending and Working Strip Iron . . 21

 III.—Simple Exercises in Bent Iron . . . 33

 IV.—Floral Ornaments for Bent Iron Work . 44

   V.—Candlesticks 50

  VI.—Hall Lanterns 59

 VII.—Screens, Grilles, etc. 78

VIII.—Table Lamps 101

 IX.—Suspended Lamps and Flower Bowls . 107

   X.—Photograph Frames 121

 XI.—Newspaper Rack 128

 XII.—Floor Lamps 131

XIII.—Miscellaneous Examples 142

     Index 157

LIST OF ILLUSTRATIONS.

FIG.	PAGE
1.—Snips	10
2.—Cutting Pliers	11
3.—Round-nosed Pliers	11
4.—Flat-nosed Pliers	12
5.—Punching Holes in Strip Iron	12
6.— Reamer	13
7.—Bench Anvil	13
8.—Bench Anvil Stake	14
9.—Block for Making Scrolls	15
10.—Iron Scroll on Block	15
11, 12.—Scroll Moulds	15
13.—Pincers for Turning Scrolls	15
14.—Fork for Bending Scrolls	16
15.—Wrench for Bending Scrolls	17
16.—Pins for Bending Scrolls	17
17 to 47.—Elementary Curves and Forms	23, 25, 27
48.—Clip for Bent Ironwork	28
49.—Cup-head Rivet	29
50.—Flat-head Rivet	29
51.—Punching Hole in Strip Iron	30
52.—Countersunk Riveting	31
53.—Cup-head Riveting	31
54.—Snap for Rounding Rivet Heads	32
55.—Lamp Bracket	34
56.—Joint for Lamp Ring	34
57.—Mounted Bowl	35
58, 59.—Scrolls for Bowl Mount	35, 36
60.—Wired Joint	36
61.—Mounted Vase	37
62.—Scrolls for Vase Mount	39
63.—Disc for Forming Conical Rings	39
64, 65.—Method of Joining Rings	39
66.—Mounted Vase	40
67.—Hanging Flower Vase	41
68.—Plan of Vase Support	41
69 to 83.—Floral Ornaments	45, 46
84, 85.—Trefoil	47, 48
86.—Lead Block in Vice Jaws	48
87.—Bracket Candlestick	50
88.—Back of Candlestick Bracket	51
89, 90.—Formation of Bosses	52
91.—Scrollwork of Candlestick Bracket Back	52
92, 93.—Candle Holder	53
94.—Table Candlestick	55

FIG.	PAGE
95.—Base and Pillar of Candlestick	55
96.—Scrolls of Candlestick	55
97, 98.—Table Candlestick	56
99.—Scrollwork of Table Candlestick	57
100, 101.—Forming Socket of Candlestick	57
102.—Bedroom Candlestick	58
103.—Underneath Plan of Candlestick	58
104.—Side Scrolls of Candlestick	58
105.—Hall Lantern	60
106.—Ball Bolt	61
107, 108.—Rings of Hall Lantern	62
109, 110.—Lamp Tray	62, 63
111.—Hall Lantern Hanger	65
112, 113.—Suspension Rods	67
114, 115.—Ornamental Hall Lantern	68
116.—Detail of Suspension Star	69
117.—Segment of Suspension Ball	69
118.—Part of Suspension Rod	70
119.—Link for Lantern Chains	70
120.—Lantern Framing	71
121, 122.—Glass and Corner of Lantern	72
123.—Securing Glass to Lantern Frame	73
124.—Corner of Lantern	73
125.—Bottom of Lantern	74
126.—Hall Lantern	75
127.—Underneath Scrolls of Hall Lantern	75
128.—Portion of Lantern Framing	76
129.—Lantern Panelling	76
130, 131.—Screen	79
132 to 135.—Riveting Framing	79, 80
136.—Scrollwork Clipped together	80
137.—Construction of Scroll	81
138.—Scrollwork of Foot of Screen	81
139.—Part of Scrollwork Filling	83
140.—Method of Fastening Glass Disc	84
141.—Grille at Winchester Cathedral	85
142, 143.—Grille Terminals	86

FIG.	PAGE
144.—Grill at Lincoln Cathedral.	86
145.—Scroll of Grille . . .	86
146.—Grille at Chichester Cathedral	88
147, 148.—Panels of Grille . .	89
149.—Eleanor Grille at Westminster Abbey . . .	89
150.—Grille at St. Denis . .	90
151.—Scroll of Grille . . .	90
152.—Grille at Santa Croce .	91
153.—Grille at Freiburg Cathedral	91
154.—Fireguard	92
155 to 157.—Details of Fireguard	93
158.—Fireguard Ornament . .	94
159 to 161.—Fireguard and Details . . . . ,	95
162, 163.—Scroll Branches and Leaves	96
164.—Firescreen	97
165.—Firescreen Standard . .	98
166.—Fixing Copper Plate in Firescreen	98
167.—Repoussé Copper Plate .	98
168.—Firescreen with Mirror Centre	99
169.—Firescreen Standard . .	100
170, 171.—Fixing Firescreen Frame	100
172.—Fixing Firescreen Mirror .	100
173.—Repoussé Brass Panel .	100
174 to 176.—Table Lamps . 102, 103
177.—Top Framework of Table Lamp	104
178.—Base of Table Lamp . .	104
179.—Section of Table Lamp Base	105
180.—Table Lamp Ornament .	105
181.—Table Lamp . . .	105
182.—Top Framework of Table Lamp	106
183.—Base of Table Lamp . .	106
184.—Suspension Lamp . .	108
185.—Ornamental Star . .	108
186.—Scrollwork	108
187.—Bracket or Wall Lamp .	109
188.—Suspended Bowl . .	111
189.—Bowl Suspension . .	111
190.—Bending Hook of Link .	111
191.—Bottom of Suspended Bowl	113
192, 193.—Incandescent Gas Hall Lamp 114, 115
194.—Oil Lamp for Hall . .	116
195, 196.—Scrolls of Hall Lamp .	117

F.G.	PAGE
197, 198.—Rosette . . .	117
199, 200.—Milled Nut and Strap	118
201, 202.—Parts of Lamp Framework	119
203.—Split Ring	119
204.—Making Twist Ornament .	119
205.—Section through Copper Rings	120
206, 207.—Double Photograph Frame 122, 123
208.—Single Photograph Frame .	124
209, 210.—Double Photograph Frame . . . 125, 126
211 to 214.—Newspaper Rack and Details 128, 129
215 to 217.—Scroll Fastening .	129
218 to 220.—Newspaper Rack Panels 129, 130
221.—Floor Lamp . . .	132
222, 223.—Floor Lamp Scrolls 132, 133
224.—Floor Lamp . . .	134
225.—Lamp Holder . . .	134
226, 227.—Lamp Shade Foundations	135
228 to 231.—Floor Lamp and Details	137
232.—Floor Lamp . . .	139
233, 234.—Foot of Lamp . .	139
235.—Floor Lamp . . .	140
236, 237.—Tripod Foot of Lamp .	141
238, 239.—Candle Sconce with Rosettes . . . 142, 143
240, 241.—Candle Sconce with Scrolls . . . 143, 144
242.—Clamp for Strip Metal .	144
243.—Scroll of Candle Sconce .	145
244.—Saucer and Candle Holder	145
245.—Rosette	145
246, 247.—Candle Holder . 145, 146
248 to 250.—Candle Sconce Saucer . . . 146, 147
251.—Brass or Copper Firescreen	147
252.—Wrought-iron Firescreen .	148
253 to 256.—Details of Firescreen	149
257, 258.—Tray Inkstand . .	150
259 to 261.—Frames of Tray Inkstand . . . 151, 152
262.—Clip at Corner of Frames .	152
263.—Scrollwork of Inkstand .	153
264.—Letter Rack . . .	154
265 to 267.—Wall Bracket . .	155
268, 269.—Joint in Wall Bracket	156

BENT IRON WORK.

CHAPTER I.

TOOLS AND MATERIALS.

BENT iron work, as a branch of amateur handicraft industry continues steadily to grow in favour. Amongst its many claims to recommendation are the following:—It is almost the only kind of metal work that can be pursued by ladies and invalids ; it is inexpensive, and the finished work is saleable at moderate prices ; it opens an extensive field for amateur design, and for an endless variety of pretty detail ; it is much more easily mastered than most amateur pastimes, than is repoussé work, for example, or wood-turning or carving, or the construction of elaborate designs in fret-work ; and much show can be made in very little time. There is practically no limit to the number of articles that may be made or ornamented with bent iron. It is applied to lamps, lanterns, vases, stands of many kinds, wall brackets, ornamental chains, candlesticks, panellings, lamp shades, screens, flower bowls, and kindred articles. There is scope not only for much variety of form, but also of colour, not only by the use of paint and varnish, but by the combination of tin, copper, and brass with iron. There is, therefore, no secret in the cause of the popularity of bent iron work, and there is little doubt but that it will become even more popular.

The metal used for the most part is narrow strips of sheet iron, of about 20 gauge. It may be had in three widths, $\frac{3}{8}$ in., $\frac{3}{16}$ in., and $\frac{1}{8}$ in. The first is employed for main frameworks, the second for minor and ornamental details, and the third for clips to hold the work together. These strips are sold in coils at from 1s. to 3s. per pound, a price that involves a heavy and an unnecessary outlay. The ordinary sheet iron from which the strips are cut can be bought in small quantities at about 3d. per pound. For those who intend to do much work in bent iron it is much cheaper in the end to purchase a stout pair of shears, and, say, half a sheet of iron, which would measure about 3 ft. by 3 ft., line it out, and cut it into strips by hand. A half-sheet would thus provide a stock of strips

Fig. 1.—Snips.

sufficient to make a large number of articles. Working in this economical fashion, the cost of material need not be great.

When the strips are cut out they should be kept ready for use by rolling them into little coils of about 3 in. diameter, and binding them with clips cut from the narrowest strips. Strips of tin plate cut from old biscuit-tins and similar articles will serve for preliminary practice, and will cost but very little.

A good variegated effect is sometimes obtained by using, in combination with iron, strips of brass and copper. These are more easily cut than iron. The sheets are sold in any gauge, and most coppersmiths will cut off pieces of any size required.

A few plain tools are necessary, but at the outside these need not cost more than 30s. The tools described below are essential. Fig. 1 shows a pair of tinmen's snips, which are used for cutting off the strips of iron to the lengths required. Pliers of various sorts and sizes are used for bending the iron. Their numbers and size will, of course, depend upon the cash available. With a wider range of tools a wider range of work can be done with less of makeshift and lost time.

A pair of cutting pliers, shown by Fig. 2, com-

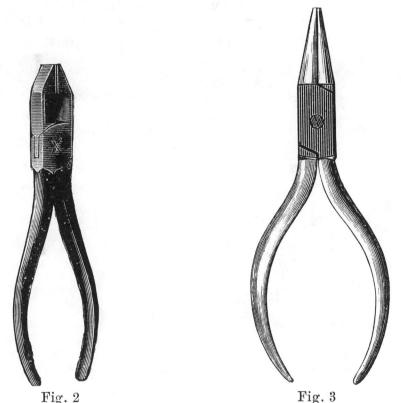

Fig. 2   Fig. 3

Fig. 2.—Cutting Pliers; Fig. 3.—Round-nosed Pliers.

prises flat jaws and a cutting edge. The latter is not required so much, because the snips serve the purpose, though the pliers are useful to cut off the narrower strips of iron if the snips do not happen to be at hand. Between the flat, roughened-up faces of the jaws short lengths of strip are flattened out and straightened, curves that are not regular are corrected, the kinks being pressed out, and one end of a strip is held while the length left free is bent to any curvature required, or waved, or twisted. The curves are imparted to the strips by means of round-nosed pliers (Fig. 3). These range from 4 in. to 8 in. in length. A single pair from 7 in. to 8 in. is the most generally useful, though a smaller pair as well comes in handy. The pliers have tapered jaws which adapts them for a slight range of curvature; but, for the most part, the

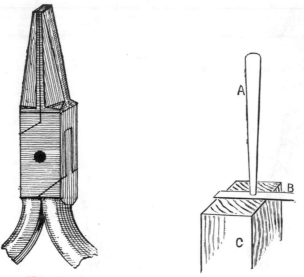

Fig. 4   Fig. 5

Fig. 4.—Flat-nosed Pliers ;   Fig. 5.—Punching Holes in Strip Iron.

curves formed do not correspond with the curvature of the pliers, being much larger, and much of the art to be acquired consists in the regular formation of these curves without their being alternately flat and curved or " kinked." The only portions whose curves correspond with those of the pliers are at the beginning of the volutes.

The flat-nosed pliers (Fig. 4) are used both for turning round the larger curves and for correcting the flatter portions that occur during their formation. They also are employed in clinching the clips by which the scrolls and other ornamental portions are secured to one another and to the

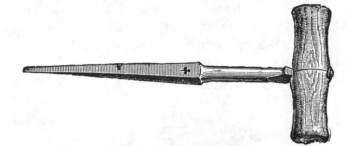

Fig. 6.—Reamer.

framings, the iron-clips being pinched between their jaws upon the work.

Common pincers are also used for a variety of purposes in the manipulation of the strips.

Holes have to be punched in the iron for rivets,

Fig. 7.—Bench Anvil.

and steel punches are used for this purpose. Those that are used for brad punches will do, being about $\frac{1}{16}$ in. in diameter at the point (Fig. 5, A). The iron strip, B, is laid upon the end grain of a block of hard wood, C, for support, while the punch is being driven through. A bench hammer weighing about

¾ lb. also is required. Fig. 6 shows a reamer that is used to broach out the punched holes.

A small bench-vice is required. A watchmaker's vice will do, but one having parallel jaws is more suitable for the heavier work of the framings. A small anvil (Fig. 7) or a stake (Fig. 8), or both of them, will also be very serviceable for bending and riveting upon.

Work is begun and held in the vice during much of the time spent upon it, and it is held so during

Fig. 8.—Bench Anvil Stake.

filing. Upon the anvil, iron strips may be flattened, and upon its beak some curved portions can be more conveniently bent and hammered than with the flat- and round-nosed pliers.

Bent iron work is well within the scope of ladies, for whose delicate hands, however, a pair of old kid gloves is almost indispensable. Without gloves the rough edges of the cut iron will scratch, and make the fingers sore. The inconvenience of working with gloves on will wear off with practice.

Bent iron work is not all mere hand bending of cold metal, and the higher branches of the art include a light form of blacksmith's work. For making scrolls of wrought iron a block (Fig. 9) is cut out of wood, or a series of wood blocks fastened one on the other, tapering upwards, the top piece having a small piece cut out of the edge for the insertion of the end of the iron to be turned. The

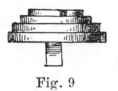

Fig. 9

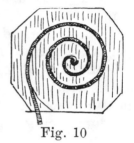

Fig. 10

Fig. 9.—Block for Making Scrolls ; Fig. 10.—Iron Scroll on Block.

block thus made, with a square pin at the bottom of the size of the square hole in the support, should be cast in iron. Fig. 10 shows the iron scroll turned round the block. When lifted off the block it will require flattening on a flat plate. Fig. 11

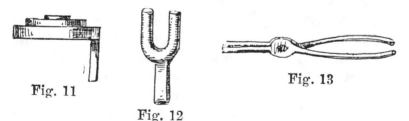

Fig. 11

Fig. 12

Fig. 13

Figs. 11 and 12.—Scroll Moulds ; Fig. 13.—Pincers for Turning Scrolls.

shows a wrought-iron scroll mould, made by turning a strong flat bar—say 1¼ in. by ½ in.—into scroll form, leaving the end down to fix into a support or in a vice. This mould must taper upwards as shown. The light iron bars are turned round this mould as round the block. Fig. 12 shows a small scroll mould made of round iron, with a square

pin to fix in a vice. The scrolls may be set to
proper shape by the use of this tool. Fig 13 shows
a pair of pincers with round jaws for the turning of
scrolls. These pincers should be made with square
jaws, half-round jaws, and also with the ends of
the jaws turned up at right angles to enable the
workman the easier to deal with the scrolls in
fitting them to their places.

A simple forked tool for use in forming scrolls
is shown by Fig. 14. A piece of iron or, better,
steel about 1 in. by ½ in., and from 6 in. to 9 in.
long, is slotted in one end about ¾ in. down and
¼ in. wide (these measurements can be modified),
the edges being slightly rounded both inside and

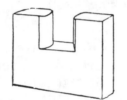

Fig. 14.—Fork for Bending Scrolls.

outside to prevent marking the soft strip metal. If
soft metal such as brass and copper is to be bent,
it will be advisable to make the fork a little stouter
in best boxwood, with a strong band of brass
driven on just below the slot to give strength.
The use of the boxwood fork prevents the scrolls
being covered with dents.

Cold iron, $\frac{1}{16}$ in. or ⅛ in. thick is not easily bent
with pliers, but with the tools shown by Fig. 15 it
will be no trouble to make the shortest of bends in
even $\frac{3}{16}$ in. cold iron. For the horn, H, take a
piece of shear or cast steel ¾ in. wide, $\frac{5}{16}$ in. thick,
and 3 in. long. Shear steel would be preferable ;
but, providing that the cast steel is not heated
beyond a bright cherry-red, it will answer very
well. Taper the ends a little by hammering or

filing, and then, ¾ in. from each end, drill or punch a $\frac{3}{16}$-in. hole. Cut out the piece from the hole to the end as shown, and open the horns a little so that they may be more readily filed up smooth and round. This done, close them in again so that one pair is ⅛ in. and the other about $\frac{3}{16}$ in. apart. Well anneal the whole article by making it red-hot and allowing it to cool slowly. The bending and punching will, of course, have to be done while the metal is hot, but an ordinary house fire will heat it sufficiently. To make the scroll wrench s, take a

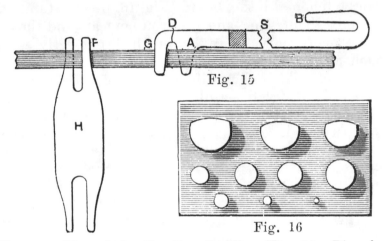

Fig. 15.

Fig. 16

Fig. 15.—Wrench for Bending Scrolls ; Fig. 16.—Pins for Bending Scrolls.

piece of steel ¾ in. wide, $\frac{5}{16}$ in. thick, and 4 in. long ; make it red-hot, then place it so that about 1 in. is over the front edge of the anvil (or any iron block with a well-rounded front edge) and hammer smartly until it is about $\frac{5}{16}$ in. square and of the shape shown at A. Punch a hole at D, ⅜ in. from the back edge, and deal with it after the manner of the horns, cutting out the piece and filing up smooth and round. Now taper the other end and bend round as at B. Anneal the whole tool thoroughly. This will be found very useful as a twisting wrench. There is no hard and fast rule in

B

using these tools, but the following will give an idea of the general method. Screw the horn H in a vice, or secure it in some way, place the iron to be bent between the prongs, put the scroll wrench on as shown, apply force, and the iron will bend between the points F and G.

Curves in thin metal can be made with tapered rods (mandrels) of wood or metal, the gradual increase in the curves being obtained by moving the work from one section of the rods to others. Also a number of short wooden pins of various curvatures can be tenoned into a board (Fig. 16, p. 18), standing up only about ½ in., and the iron bent around these. Very many curves can be finished perfectly with such an appliance. The pins also afford a ready means of testing the uniform accuracy of a number of similar curved scrolls. Again, when finishing the small ends of scrolls it is better, when the terminal curve is very small, not to turn it completely with the wire pliers, which are liable to produce kinks. It is better to insert the small end of a mandrel and pinch the terminal curve round it with the flat-nosed pliers.

If a black polished surface is required on bent iron work, the surface must be smoothed down, and then painted with cycle enamel. A good dead black paint for ornamental ironwork may be prepared by mixing well together 7 lb. of pure drop black ground in turpentine, with ½ pt. japan gold size, thinned down to proper consistency with American turpentine ; this dries hard with a dead black finish, and thus differs from Berlin black. This paint, if properly mixed in the manner described above, is not affected by the weather ; the gold size is added to bind the black and prevent it rubbing up, and is also a protection against the weather. Drop black, if obtained pure, is one of the most permanent of the black pigments.

Ornamental ironwork is often prepared by heating it and then dipping it into a small tank of a good quality Berlin black; this leaves on the ironwork a thin film of dull black, which adheres firmly and should be quite durable providing that the Berlin black is of a good quality.

A chemical method of obtaining a dull black finish on small iron articles is as follows:—After removing thoroughly all grease and dirt, the iron may be painted with, or dipped into, a solution consisting of 1 part bismuth chloride, 2 parts mercury bichloride, 1 part copper chloride, 6 parts hydrochloric acid, 5 parts alcohol, and 50 parts water, well stirred together. When dry, place in boiling water, and keep boiling for half an hour. Should the colour not be dark or black enough, repeat the operation. The black is fixed by coating with boiled oil and heating till all oil is driven off.

The brass and copper with which bent iron work is ornamented require to be lacquered. The articles to be lacquered first are thoroughly cleaned by dipping in diluted sulphuric acid and rinsing in clean water, so that the colour of the metal is fully exposed. They are then laid on a stove (a sheet of iron with a gas-jet beneath it being sufficient for small articles) and heated, but they should not be made so hot as to colour the metal. When hot enough, which must be found by trial, apply the lacquer with a camel-hair brush. If the right temperature has been attained, there should be a slight hissing when the lacquer is applied. Reheat the lacquered article and then allow to cool; the lacquered surface must not, while it is hot, be touched with the fingers.

Lacquer suitable for brass work is made easily by dissolving best pale shellac in cold spirit of wine, and colouring it with gamboge, saffron, or dragon's blood, according to the tint required. The following are recipes for brass lacquers. (1) Put into 1 pt. of alcohol 1 oz. of turmeric powder, 2 dr. of annatto, and 2 dr. of saffron. Shake well during seven days and strain into a clean bottle. Now add 3 oz. of clean shellac and shake during another fourteen days. (2) ½ oz. of gamboge, 1½ oz. of aloes, 8 oz. of shellac, and 1 gal. of spirit of wine. (3) Seed lac, dragon's blood, annatto, and gamboge, of each 4 oz., 1 oz. of saffron, and 10 pt. of spirit of wine. (4) 3 oz. of seed lac, 2 oz. of amber, 2 oz. of gamboge, ½ dr. of extract of red sanders, 1 dr. of dragon's blood, ½ dr. of saffron, and 2¼ pt. of spirit of wine.

For a gold lacquer for tin, get methylated spirit 1 gal., gum sandarach 1 lb., and aniline yellow (soluble in spirit) 1 oz. Place the gum in a stoppered bottle with the spirit, and agitate at intervals until the gum is thoroughly dissolved. The aniline yellow is then added, the liquid is again stirred, and is then passed through a fine strainer, when the lacquer is ready for use.

A bright (cold) gold lacquer for brass and tin that will cover solder marks may be made by dissolving 1 lb. of ground turmeric, 1½ oz. of gamboge, 3½ lb. of powdered gum sandarach, and ¾ lb. of shellac in 2 gal. of spirit of wine. When shaken, dissolved, and strained, add 1 pt. of turpentine varnish.

The following is a recipe for a lacquer that will give to tin the colour of brass. Take 3 oz. of seed lac, 2 dr. of dragon's blood, and 1 oz. of turmeric powder, and place in 1 pt. of well rectified spirit. Allow to remain thus for fourteen days, but give the bottle a shaking up at least once each day. When thoroughly well combined, strain the liquid through muslin. The tinware to be coloured must be dipped in dilute acid to remove all dirt and grease, and dried in warm sawdust, when it is ready for the lacquer to be brushed over it in the ordinary way.

CHAPTER II.

MOST of the elementary forms of curves used in bent iron work are shown in the three groups, Figs. 17 to 27, p. 23 ; Figs. 28 to 35, p. 25 ; and Figs. 36 to 47, p. 27. They are not numerous, but are turned in many sizes and united in many combinations. Before attempting to construct any design in bent iron work, it is better to devote a few hours to practice in bending these elementary forms.

For bending any of the volute or scroll forms in Figs. 17 to 39, proceed as follows : Take the strip in the left hand, or in the jaws of the flat-nose pliers held in the left hand, and with the round-nosed pliers in the right hand twist the free end of the iron into the small curve, then with the pliers work gradually outwards, forming in detail the enlarging curves of the volute, and so diminishing down to the small curves at the other end.

The difficulty in this bending is to form flowing curves without flats or kinks. Work very deliberately, not trying to bend too much at once, and, where practicable, use a templet. The small curves, whose diameters correspond pretty closely with the diameter of the pliers, are easily done ; the difficulty lies in the flatter ones. The flatter parts should, therefore, be bent by a succession of slight movements of the pliers, a very slight bending of the iron being imparted in each position of the pliers. Or, instead, one of the bending appliances described in Chapter I. can be used.

The advantage of thus bending the work is that the iron being so thin, all flats can be pinched out and good curves ultimately produced; but a great deal of time is wasted thus, so that it is better to learn the art of producing perfect curves at once, even though the process may seem tedious until practice has produced skill.

The curve shown by Fig. 20 is one of the ornaments that occur plentifully, being fastened to the bigger curves by clips (shown enlarged by Fig. 48, p. 28).

Turning now to the C-shaped scroll (Fig. 21), it will be noticed that this form also can be changed according to requirements. A great deal can be done by making a "heart" or C scroll "open" or "close." For close work, or where a choice design is required in a small space, Fig. 24 is effective. Try the effect of bending a scroll back upon itself to a hook shape (Fig. 26). Sometimes a very simple thing is required, and if the curl at each end is left off, and a sharp bend is used instead of a round one, the result is the Greek letter Omega (Fig. 25). Now add a small curl, and the result (Fig. 27) is much more pleasing. Of course, a scroll must not be judged by itself, unless it is to be used singly. The art of scroll designing lies in the ability to combine simple bends in such a manner as to produce the most pleasing results. Returning to the class of scrolls shown in Fig. 26, the bending in the reverse direction may take place in the initial stage of its formation. Bend the end of the strip that is to become a scroll into a semicircle, and then bend it in the opposite direction and finish as a C scroll. The result is shown in Fig. 22. The process may also be applied to S-shaped scrolls, as in Fig. 38, p. 27.

The curves in Figs. 28 and 29 are slightly modified in form, but they are very useful and very common. Figs. 34 and 37 are leaves, and are most easily bent. The centre of Fig. 34 is filled in with a midrib and scrolls; these are frequently formed of

Figs. 17 to 27.—Elementary Curves.

copper. For the tendrils (Fig. 41) the iron is simply bent backward and forward with the wire pliers. Figs. 40 and 46 are tendrils of a different type, that lie closer to their scrolls than does that shown by Fig. 41. Figs. 32 and 35 are suspension chains, formed by twisting the iron continuously in one direction with two pairs of pliers. Figs. 42 and 43 show double curves, extensively used in ornamentation. Fig. 30 is a chain link. Fig. 47 is an ornamental border, for use round a panelled design.

A simple S scroll has the same shape at both ends ; if cut in halves it is found useful to fill corners and can be used in combination with others. An unequal-ended scroll is shown by Fig. 36 ; its uses are different from those of the simple scroll. A sharp bend introduced into an S scroll will vary the effects considerably. Thus, if a long S scroll is bent over at a sharp angle, the result is shown in Fig. 44. The effect of another bend is shown by Fig. 45, and the effect of bending both ends in the same direction is illustrated by Fig. 33, which, though not possessing great charm by itself, will yet be useful at times. For instance, Fig. 31 shows two such scrolls placed together.

The application of the forms will be explained fully in subsequent chapters ; but before attempting to make any of the articles there described the beginner should practise the bending of simple curves and outlines.

Some of the principal elementary operations involved in the construction of the heavier portions of bent iron work will be here considered.

Bent iron work consists of two portions, the framing or skeleton, and the ornamental parts. Many amateurs purchase the framings, and do only the ornamental work themselves, but this is expensive, and not satisfactory, and the amateur can do the entire work himself, for the sections of iron are not heavy. There is very little indeed over

about $\frac{1}{8}$ in. and $\frac{3}{16}$ in. square, and about $\frac{3}{8}$ in. in
width by $\frac{1}{8}$ in. in thickness; and all this can be
easily heated to a redness in a kitchen fire, and bent

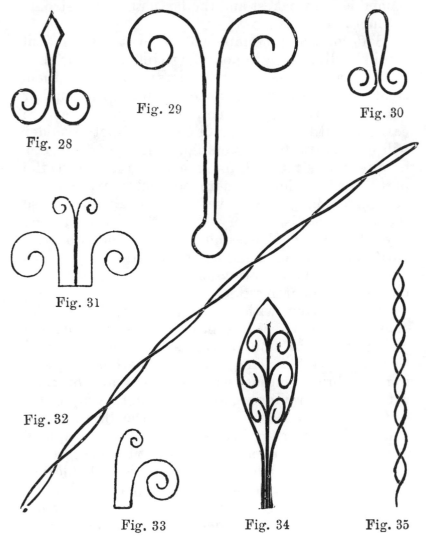

Figs. 28 to 35.—Elementary Curves and Forms.

over a small anvil or in the vice. Welding is not
at all necessary, so the forge operations on the larger
sections are simply those of bending, and occasional
tapering or thinning down, as will be made clear.

The three methods of uniting the heavier framings which support the bent iron work ornamentation are soldering, brazing, and riveting. The first named is the weakest and the last named the strongest method.

Soft soldering is employed in positions where it would be difficult or impossible to introduce the clips (Fig. 48) and the nose of the pliers for pinching them tightly. Many such instances occur in the smaller curves, whereas the fastenings of large curves are easily got at. In very small curves a spot of solder will effect a perfect fastening ; and indeed there is no alternative method, for if solder is not used, the parts must be left in mere contact only, without any fastening. This is very undesirable, because the bent iron is so very slight that it should be strengthened at all possible points. The two principal methods of soft soldering—the copper-bit method and the sweating-on method—are each employed in bent iron work.

In soldering with the copper-bit, before the ends are actually secured in place, just the surfaces which are to be united with solder must be filed clean and bright. They are tied together with soft iron- or brass-binding wire, or they are pinched with clamps or pincers, or kept together by other suitable means. Run in between the bright faces a little killed spirits of salts ; this is the raw spirits in which zinc has been dissolved until effervescence ceases. Water is added, and this is called chloride of zinc or soldering fluid. In the right hand have a copper-bit, properly tinned and heated just below redness, and a stick of solder in the left ; melt a portion of the solder with the bit, letting it run between the surfaces to be joined. The solder will follow the soldering fluid, and set firm in an instant. This is a method well suited to a number of small points of contact.

Sweating-on is preferable for large surfaces,

Figs. 36 to 47.—Elementary Curves and Forms.

which first are cleaned with a file, then moistened with the prepared soldering fluid, and a thin layer of solder is melted and worked over each surface smooth and level with one of the flat bevelled faces of the copper-bit. The two surfaces are then brought into contact, pinched together, and heated up to the melting point of the solder, when the two soldered surfaces will unite. The requisite heat may be obtained from a clear fire, or from a Bunsen flame, or from a pair of red-hot tongs, used for pinching the parts together.

Brazing, or hard soldering, is accomplished either with a blowpipe flame or in a clear fire. File clean the surfaces to be united, and tie the parts together with iron binding wire, or with soft brass wire. If

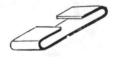

Fig. 48.—Clip for Bent Iron Work.

the latter is used, it supplies the solder or spelter. If soft iron wire is used for binding, then special spelter is employed; it is sold in various qualities which melt at different temperatures so as to suit different metals and alloys; but almost any spelter will do for uniting iron. The spelter is in grains; these are mixed with powdered borax, which serves as a flux, and with water, and then placed on the edges of the work. The borax should be fused first to drive off its water of crystallisation, otherwise it will swell upon the work and displace the spelter. The mixture of spelter, borax, and water is taken up with a spoon, and placed upon the edge of the joint; and when the temperature has been raised sufficiently in the fire or in the blowpipe flame, the spelter and borax will melt and run between the joints. At once remove the work from the heat, and when cold file the edges smooth, as brazing leaves the work rough.

Riveting light work is very simple. There are two kinds of rivets—the cup-head or snap (Fig. 49), and the flat or countersunk head (Fig. 50); either may be used. For thin iron the cup-head rivet is best, because the hole has not to be countersunk, the countersinking weakening the weak iron very much. The flat head, unless it is countersunk, standing up above the iron, keen and jagged, looks unsightly. The cup-head rivet, on the other hand, forms a neat finish to the work. In some instances, where it is desirable that the surfaces shall be perfectly level, then the holes must be countersunk, and the best

Fig. 49   Fig. 50

Fig. 49.—Cup-head Rivet; Fig. 50.—Flat-head Rivet.

job possible made of it. In the heavier framings— say, of $\frac{1}{16}$ in. thick and over—this is readily done.

Rivets more than $\frac{1}{8}$ in. in diameter are but seldom required for framings, and for most work $\frac{1}{16}$-in. rivets are large enough. They may be of iron or copper.

The holes for the rivets are more quickly punched than drilled in the thinnest iron, but in metal more than $\frac{1}{16}$ thick they must be drilled.

To punch a hole in thin iron, the strip may be laid upon the end grain of a block of hard wood, as shown in Fig. 5, p. 12. A steel punch, flat at its round cutting end, but made keen at the edges by touching the end on the grindstone, is then driven through with a single blow of a hammer. The disc which is punched out will become embedded in the wood, and the support afforded by the hard wood will prevent the formation of much burr. What there is will be filed off or hammered back, and the hole reamed out with the tool shown by Fig. 6, p. 13.

Another and better way of punching holes is shown in Fig. 51, in which A is a piece of bar steel,

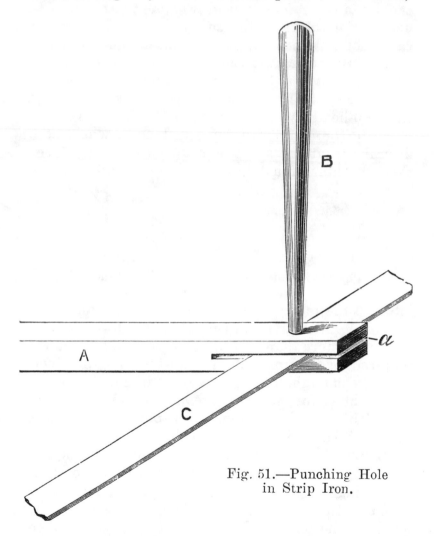

Fig. 51.—Punching Hole in Strip Iron.

having a narrow slit, *a*, cut at one end with a hack-saw. The steel punch, B, passes through a hole drilled right through the bar from one face to the other. The iron strip, C, is passed through the slit and adjusted, and a single blow of the punch upon it forms the hole, and the disc passes through the bottom part of the hole in the bar, A. This makes a keen, clean hole, and there is no need to use file or reamer for finishing it, because the strip, c, has a better bedding upon the iron than it would have upon a wood block.

For drilling holes in thicker iron, practically any form of drill may be employed. One of the common archimedean drill-stocks is useful for general work, and it has this great advantage—that it can be used on work which is in course of construction, in any position, and at any angle.

The actual process of riveting is carried out in the following way : Obtain a rivet of such a length that, when it is inserted through the holes in the two strips which it has to connect, the tail shall

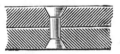

Fig. 52   Fig. 53

Fig. 52.—Countersunk Riveting; Fig. 53.—Cup-head Riveting.

project for a distance equal to about one and a quarter times its own diameter. That is to say, a $\frac{1}{16}$-in. rivet should project about $\frac{5}{64}$ in.—a very full $\frac{1}{16}$ in.—whilst a $\frac{1}{8}$-in. rivet should project about $\frac{5}{32}$ in. A firm bedding is obtained, such as that afforded by a small anvil or block of iron, or even by the top of the vice-jaw ; and upon this the head of the rivet is laid while the tail is hammered over, using the narrow cross-peen of the hammer ; the hammer must not weigh more than about $\frac{1}{2}$ lb., and should be of good quality. The aim of the blows is to spread the metal ; therefore they are delivered, not only vertically, but also sideways, in order to drive the metal outwards. This must be done equally and gradually, so that the spreading-out shall not become one-sided, nor the metal split, nor simply bent over. Several dozen blows will have to be delivered on a small rivet.

For countersunk rivets (Fig. 50) the battered end is simply filed off flush with the surface of the strips, as in Fig. 52; the cup-head rivets are finished as in

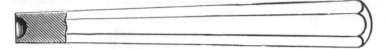

Fig. 54.—Snap for Rounding Rivet Heads.

Fig. 53 by means of a special tool, called a snap (Fig. 54). This merely is a piece of steel rod cupped out at one end to a semicircular form, and hardened. The hollowed end fits over the tail end of the rivet, and two or three blows upon the head of the tool will finish the rivet neatly.

CHAPTER III.

SIMPLE EXERCISES IN BENT IRON.

A SKETCH of a simple lamp bracket is given by Fig. 55. Begin the construction of this by forming the large scroll B D, and make the bends by the method found the easiest. If the steel fork shown by Fig. 14, p. 16, is used, place the strip of $\frac{1}{2}$-in. by $\frac{1}{8}$-in. iron in it, with just the end projecting, and beat it sideways with a hammer, letting more of the iron project as the metal bends. When the first 5 in. or 6 in. have been curled up, beginning, of course, at D (Fig. 55), the fork will be all that is necessary for bending the remaining portion. With soft iron there will be but little difficulty in getting a good bend, but should the metal prove stubborn it must be well annealed by bringing to red heat and cooling very slowly. When using the fork, work methodically, always beginning at the inside. Do not bend the scroll in bits, as it were, but beginning at the inside gradually work along the scroll, not passing a bit anywhere that is not perfect.

For the scroll A B, cut off sufficient metal, and begin as before, but with more care, because the bends are smaller, particularly at B. Make a neat job where the two scrolls join, as a gap looks unworkmanlike. The next job is to make the ring to carry the vessel of the lamp. To get the circumference of this, multiply the diameter by $3\frac{1}{7}$, and add an allowance for the thickness of the metal. Now in regard to joining the ring, the quickest and simplest way is to braze it, but the following device is quite effectual:—Cut the metal strip

C

about $\frac{3}{4}$ in. too long, and file both of the ends for $\frac{3}{4}$ in. to half their thickness, and then bend to form the ring. The joint, which afterwards is riveted at c, is shown by Fig. 56.

The back rod needs scarcely any description. It is of $\frac{1}{2}$-in. solid iron, tapered at the bottom. The eyes are made from flat $\frac{1}{4}$-in. by $\frac{3}{4}$-in. iron, and are intended to be driven into the wall. The top

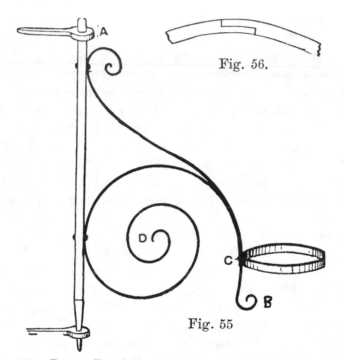

Fig. 56.

Fig. 55

Fig. 55.—Lamp Bracket; Fig. 56.—Joint of Lamp Ring.

eye is drilled so that the rod will slip through, but the bottom one is made to fit about half-way up the taper, which must be fairly gradual. If the bottom eye and the taper are carefully fitted this will be sufficient to prevent the lamp swinging, except when pressure is applied.

Drill holes at the places shown, drilling the ring at the joint, and fix the whole together by rivets. If the holes are well countersunk the rivets may be

filed off level, and thus there will be nothing to
show how the pieces are joined. To finish, file the
whole smooth, and give it a couple of coats of
dead black paint.

Mounts for a glass bowl and for some vases may

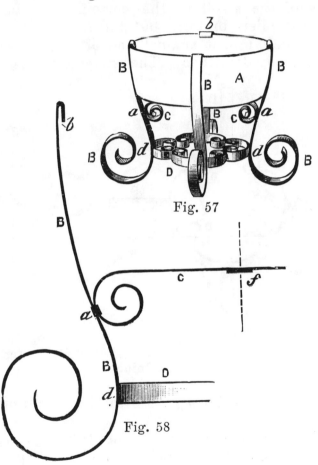

Fig. 57

Fig. 58

Fig. 57.—Mounted Bowl; Fig. 58.—Scrolls of Bowl Mount.

be made, and general designs for these and the
same methods of construction will also serve for
vases of other forms and sizes.

Fig. 57 illustrates a glass bowl, A, suitable for
holding flowers or ferns. It is supported with
four legs, B, shown enlarged by Fig. 58. A plan

of the underneath scrolls is given by Fig. 59, and the method of tying the strips to each other is shown by Fig. 60.

For the legs prepare four scrolls, B, from the ordinary thin iron strips $\frac{3}{8}$ in. wide. The quick turns of the scroll at the bottom must be bent with the pliers or fork, but the flat curves above can be better bent against one of the flat wooden pins already described. The extreme end is turned

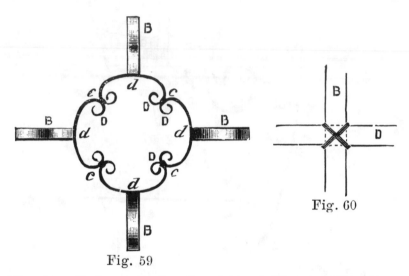

Fig. 59

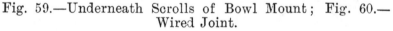

Fig. 59.—Underneath Scrolls of Bowl Mount; Fig. 60.— Wired Joint.

over at b to fall down within the bowl, clipping its edge.

The bowl is supported by, and the strips, B, tied at the bottom of the bowl to, the two strips, C, C, which are carried straight underneath the bowl if the bottom is flat, or suitably curved if the bottom is convex. They cross each other at the centre (f, Fig. 58), and may be fastened to each other there with a spot of solder, though this is not essential. Then, where C abuts against B (Fig. 58), they are secured with clips, a, of bent iron, pinched fast with the flat-nosed pliers.

The mounting may be considered complete at this stage if time is a consideration; but the stand will be steadier if the circle of double scrolls, D, is added. These scrolls will prevent the legs, B, from spreading outwards, and the curves will form a neat filling-in beneath the bowl, relieving it of the meagre appearance which it would otherwise have. There are four scrolls in the figure, and they are

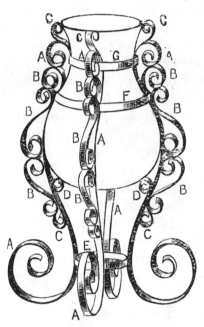

Fig. 61.—Mounted Vase.

clipped to each other at c and fastened to the legs at d, either with solder or with fine soft iron or copper wire, as shown in Fig. 60. This completes the mounting, which then should be blacked or varnished.

A vase mounted on four legs is illustrated by Fig. 61. One of these legs, with its attachments, is shown enlarged by Fig. 62. The whole of the work is made of $\frac{3}{8}$-in. strips.

The main strips which form the legs, A, are bent to the scroll form at bottom and top with

pliers ; the flat curve in the body is bent round
a suitable templet block of wood. The first leg
being made accurately, the other three are tested
by it, until all four are uniform in shape and size.
Or they can be tried upon a full-sized drawing;
for it is always desirable before commencing any-
thing in bent iron to mark the outlines full size
upon a black-board with chalk, or upon a chalked
board with pencil or crayon.

The scrolls, B, three to each leg, are then bent,
and fastened to the legs, A, with clips at a, a,
and to each other at b. Also two small scrolls, c,
at top and bottom, are clipped to A ; the lower
one also is clamped at b to B. Note that when-
ever double curves occur in bent iron, as at the
parting, b , two strips are required to form them,
because a single strip cannot be divided by bifurca-
tion. This is shown clearly in Fig. 62.

The four legs, with their scrolls, having been
prepared, are fastened around the vase by means
of two cross strips, D, D, and three rings, E, F, G.
The cross strips, D, are bent to fit the bottom of the
vase, which they support, and are formed into
scrolls at the ends and united to the legs, A, at c,
with clips.

The bottom ring, E, is bent round into a circle,
either to a line struck with compasses, or around
the edge of a wooden disc, and its ends are over-
lapped for a length of about ⅜ in., and soldered.
It is fastened to the four legs, either with solder
or with soft iron wire, as in Fig. 60.

The rings, F and G, are made differently. F
forms a frustrum of a cone—very narrow, it is true,
but, nevertheless, sufficiently conical to give some
trouble in the setting out. Its form could be
developed and cut out of thin iron, but this would
give trouble also, which might be saved in making
it in copper, which can be hammered to almost any
form with ease. The strip of copper, bent round

as a parallel ring, can be hammered to the correct form around a disc of hard wood (Fig. 63), with its edges shaped to the required bevel. The copper band will contrast well with the iron; indeed, all

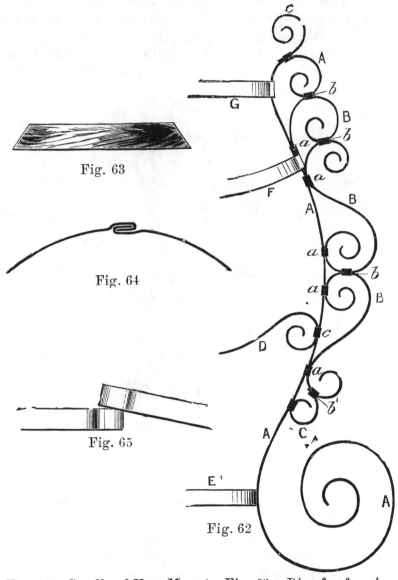

Fig. 63

Fig. 64

Fig. 65

Fig. 62

Fig. 62.—Scrolls of Vase Mount; Fig. 63.—Disc for forming Conical Rings; Figs. 64 and 65.—Method of Joining Rings.

the bands might well be of copper. When copper is used only because of its superior ductility, and a uniform black is desirable, it can be varnished to match the black iron.

The upper ring, G, is a parallel zone, and may be made easily in iron. Though the bottom ring, E, is in contact with the inside faces of the legs, A. it is better that F and G should encircle A. It is possible to fasten these rings to A with wire, in the

Fig. 66.—Mounted Vase.

same way as that shown by Fig. 60 ; but it is tedious, and does not make a neat job, because it is impossible to make the rings embrace the legs tightly by this method.

A better method of fastening the rings is to take the diameter accurately, and then turn over the ends to make a tinman's seam-joint (Fig. 64) ; then embrace the legs, bring the ends over one another (see Fig. 65), and slip the two parts to-

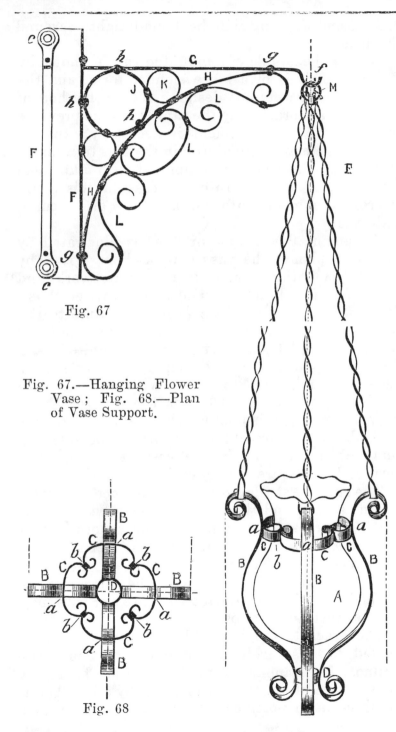

Fig. 67

Fig. 67.—Hanging Flower Vase ; Fig. 68.—Plan of Vase Support.

Fig. 68

gether, and the ring will be bound tightly around
the legs.

A second example of a mounted vase is shown by
Fig. 66. This is of a more slender form, and the
mount is of a different design. As the method of
making this is practically the same as in the previous
case, scarcely any comment is necessary. In this
instance the main strip of iron in the legs terminates
at A A, and the legs are completed with additional
curves, B, C, and D. In every case in this figure
where curves come into contact they are secured
with a clip.

A hanging flower vase or bowl is illustrated by
Fig. 67, a plan of the vase support being given by
Fig. 68. A is the vase, B, C, D its framework, and
F its supporting bracket. The vase is carried thus:
Four enclosing ribs, B, are all curved alike to the
outline illustrated, using wire pliers and suitably
swept templet-pins. The ribs are united, and
the vase suspended by the four double scrolls, C;
the scrolls are united to B at a with fine iron wire
(as illustrated by Fig. 60); or the opposed faces
may, of course, be soldered, this being the neater
method. Make sure of the security of the soldered
joints before trusting fragile vases to them; but
these flat joints are very simple.

The ring, D, at the bottom, is fastened to B with
wire or solder, and then the vase may be inserted,
and the curves, C, fastened to one another with
clips at b. The ribs, B, and curves, C, easily can
be opened out sufficiently to permit of the insertion of the vase, and with care the clips may be
pinched at b without injuring the vase; or wire may
be used instead of clips.

The bracket, F, from which the vase is suspended, has a severely simple and quite elementary
outline. Its framing is made of iron, having a
cross section of about $\frac{3}{8}$ in. or $\frac{5}{16}$ in. by $\frac{1}{8}$ in. There
are three main portions—the back F, top G, and

diagonal H. F is flattened at the ends, c, and drilled to receive screws for fastening the bracket to the wall. G is turned up and is riveted to F and bent at the other end, f, to form a suspension hook; H is curved, and riveted to F and G at g, g.

With regard to the scroll work, the ring, J, made of the same section of iron as the framing, acts as a stiffener, preventing H from yielding inwards under pressure. It is riveted at h, h, h. All the rest of the work, the small rings, K, and the scrolls, L, L, may be made of the thin iron strips, and clips (as shown) will be employed for holding them fast together.

For suspending the vase are shown imitation chains, made of bent iron, twisted as illustrated by Fig. 35, p. 25. Each length of iron, after having been twisted, is turned over at each end, and is brought underneath the top curve of B at one end, and at the other is slipped into a ring, M. The four rings, M, are slung on the hook, f, and sustain the vase.

CHAPTER IV.

FLORAL ORNAMENTS FOR BENT IRON WORK.

FLORAL ornaments, executed chiefly in copper, are largely used to embellish bent iron work. Copper flowers are among the most common of these ornaments. They are in quite a conventional fashion. Little discs of thin copper (about 20 B.W.G.) are cut out either to a truly circular form (Fig. 69, or with shallow waved margins (Fig. 70), or with deeply dentated margins to represent petals (Figs. 71 and 72). A slit or a hole is punched in the middle of each, and then the copper is hammered into a hemispherical, or a nearly hemispherical, form, upon a cake of hard pitch; or if there are a good many flowers of the same size required, a concave mould of hard wood, or of metal, may be used, and a punch with a convex end of the same size as the concavity of the flower may also be used to save time, and the flower will be smoother, cleaner, and more free from bruises if so made. The central part of the flower, in this case supposed to represent stamens, is formed of a flat bit of thin copper (Fig. 73), and the stem is a prolongation of this, and passes through the slit punched in the disc. Of course this is very conventional indeed, but nevertheless the grouping of these rude copper flowers is very effective among the black iron. More elaborate ones, however, will be shown. They have flat stems which can be clipped with less trouble than those of round wire between the flat iron curves.

Slightly modified forms, a few of many designs

possible, are shown by Figs. 74 to 77. Of course, in these ornaments there must be a good deal of conventional or formal treatment; but the main thing is good effect, and this can be obtained in such forms and by variation in colour. The petals are made from sheet copper, tin, or iron. If made

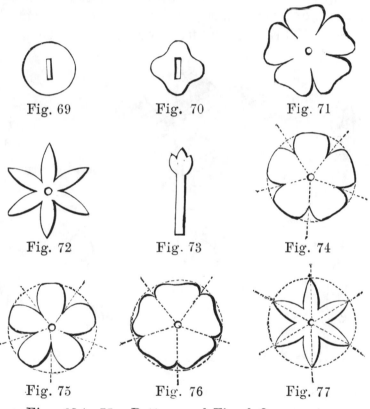

Fig. 69   Fig. 70   Fig. 71

Fig. 72   Fig. 73   Fig. 74

Fig. 75   Fig. 76   Fig. 77

Figs. 69 to 77.—Patterns of Floral Ornaments.

of copper, they are left of their natural colour; if of tin or iron, they are coated with a dead-black varnish. The original circles from which the rays of petals are cut are shown by the dotted circles. In each case there are five petals, and the circles are therefore divided into five equal parts, which correspond with the divisions between the petals, or else with their centre lines—it does not matter

which. Figs. 74 and 75 are similar, but the latter
is cut more deeply. Figs. 76 and 77 are of different
types. In each of these instances a single circle of
petals only may be used to form a flower, or,
alternately, several such may be superimposed,
with their cleft portions alternating. In this case
the upper sets of petals should be cleft more deeply
than the lower ones, or else be cut to smaller
circles. Three, four, five, or six may be super-

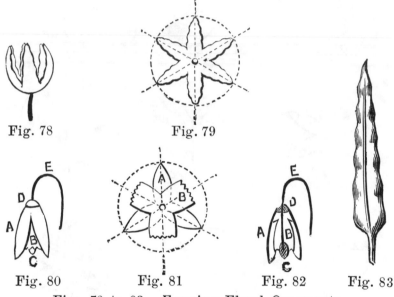

Fig. 78　　　　　　　Fig. 79

Fig. 80　　　　Fig. 81　　　　Fig. 82　　　Fig. 83

Figs. 78 to 83.—Forming Floral Ornaments.

imposed in this fashion with good effect. Some
amount of concavity must be imparted to each
disc and to each separate petal, the amount being
varied according as they are in an upper or lower
series—more in the upper, less in the lower—or
according as the flowers are required to appear—
full-blown or partly opened. A round-faced steel
punch is used to impart the concavity, the metal
being laid upon a block of pitch or of compo, such
as is used in repoussé work. Observe that a hole
is punched or drilled in the centre of each circle.

Through this the petals are secured in their super-imposed positions, copper or iron wire being passed through the holes. A central boss is required in this flower to represent the disc of the composite flowers, or the ovary-case, etc., of other kinds. This may be formed neatly by soldering an ordinary rivet-head, like those used in model work, upon the end of the copper or iron wire ; or a spot of solder may be run upon the end in the centre of the petals, and rounded up neatly. In the case of flowers

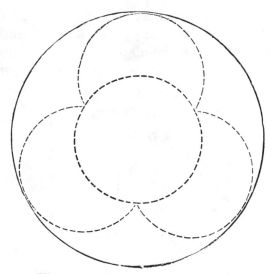

Fig. 84.—Pattern for Trefoil.

with long projecting stamens and anthers, these may be formed with small nails, or with pins soldered into the boss representing the seed-case. Other ways will suggest themselves to the worker.

Another form of floral ornament is shown by Fig. 78. It is formed by cutting deep petals (Fig. 79) with waved edges, and bending these up as shown in Fig. 78. An ovary and stamens will be formed in the manner just described.

Another ornament is shown at Fig. 80. Petals A and B (Fig. 81) are cut separately into conventional outlines, and are bent or dished into concave forms ; Fig. 82 is a section, Fig. 80 giving an external view of the flower. A pistil, C, is formed with solder or other suitable means, and a calyx, D, similarly. The latter, if made of solder, serves

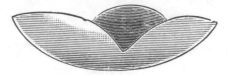

Fig. 85.—Shaped Trefoil.

to secure the copper wire, E, in the centre of the petals. For rosettes, see pp. 56, 82, 118, and 146.

Conventional leaves also are largely used, and they are very easily made. A narrow lanceolate form, suitable for combination with floral orna-

Fig. 86.—Lead Block in Vice Jaws.

ment, is shown in Fig. 83. It is cut from copper, or tin, or iron, and the waviness or concavity required is imparted on a pitch-block, as in the case of flowers. Other kinds are shown by Figs. 162 and 163, p. 96.

To make copper trefoils, cut out eight discs of sheet copper, 2 in. in diameter, and with a pair of compasses mark out the trefoil pattern as shown by Fig. 84. Cut out with snips, and finish and smooth the edges with file and emery-cloth. To shape these as indicated by Fig. 85, get a block of lead—this is indispensable to the art metal worker —about 5 in. by 6 in. by 2 in., and of the shape suggested by the sectional view, Fig. 86, so that it may be firmly fitted in a vice. With the round peen of a riveting hammer makes a slight circular hollow about the size of a sixpence near the edge of the lead block, and holding the leaf portion of the copper trefoil over this indentation, beat it down with the round end of a hammer. In this way the trefoil may be shaped easily, and by slight hammering over a larger, but shallow, concavity in the lead, the whole may be evenly hollowed as illustrated by Fig. 85.

CHAPTER V.

CANDLESTICKS.

CANDLESTICKS are not used so much now as formerly; but they are retained for bedroom service, and as they can be made very prettily in bent iron, it is proposed to illustrate a few forms.

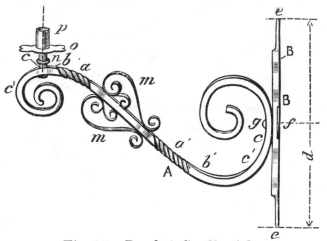

Fig. 87.—Bracket Candlestick.

The bracket candlestick illustrated by Figs. 87 and 88 is suitable for screwing-up against the head of a bed or to a wall. The main framework, A and B, is of iron rod, $\frac{1}{4}$ in. square in section; the remainder is of thin strips, $\frac{1}{4}$ in. wide. Draw the entire bracket to a convenient size, measure round the curves of A with string or wire to get the length of rod required. Cut off a rod and heat one of the parts ag to a white heat; hold the bar at b or b' with tongs or pincers, and with another pair of tongs turn the bar round and round, and so form the twist, *a*; repeat this operation at the other section, *a*. Heat the parts *c c* for about 1 in. or 1½ in. of length, one at a time, and upset them by striking the end of the bar upon a lump of iron, which will, of course, thicken or dump the metal up at the heated section. An elementary acquaintance with working metals by heat, as gained from the companion handbook, "Smiths' Work," will be found exceedingly useful here. Flatten out the metal with the hammer in the width-way of the bar, thus giving it the appear-

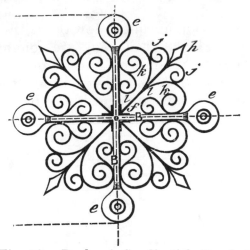

Fig. 88.—Back of Candlestick Bracket.

ance of Fig. 89. Heat it again, and punch a hole in the centre (Fig. 90). The bar will next be bent to the scroll forms shown by *c' c'*, in Fig. 87. It will be raised to a moderate red-heat and hammered gently around the beak of the anvil, or round any suitable curved surface of metal, or even bent with tongs. The bar will be tried from time to time upon the full-sized drawing, and its curves set and corrected with the hammer, until all flats and angularities are removed, and good flowing scrolls obtained.

The back of candlestick is illustrated by Fig. 88.

The cross, B, is made thus : Take two strips, each, say, 1 in. longer than the total distance, d, over the bosses, e e, Fig. 87. Heat the ends of each in succession to a white heat, and upset by hammering or by dumping down upon the face of a

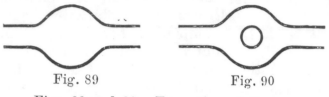

Fig. 89   Fig. 90

Figs. 89 and 90.—Formation of Bosses.

block of iron. Spread out sideways with the hammer, and thin down until they are roughly of the form of the bosses shown, and then file up to correct shape. Drill and countersink the screw-holes in the centres of e, and weld the bars, B, at the centre, where they cross each other. To do this, upset them slightly, raise to the welding heat, lay them across each other at right angles, and strike

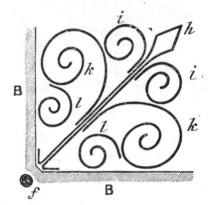

Fig. 91.—Scrollwork of Candlestick Bracket Back.

smartly until their faces are flush on both sides. Neatly file off the metal about the centre to form a little boss, and in the centre of this punch or drill a rivet-hole, f. Through this the rivet, g, which unites the scroll, A, to the back, B, is put. To prevent the scroll from turning round on the rivet, make this very fast, or file out the hole square, and make the shank of the rivet to agree, or run a little solder round it.

The bent iron work on the back, B (Figs. 87 and 88), is made in four similar portions. The separate parts of one quatrefoil are shown separate by Fig. 91, the letters agreeing with Fig. 88. First, the cen-

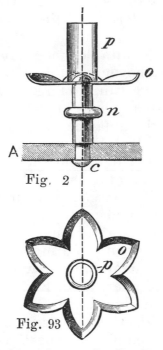

Fig. 2

Fig. 93

Figs. 92 and 93.—Candle Holder.

tral finial, *h*, is bent round upon itself, and turned backwards at the ends, to be soldered or clamped to B. To *h* the flanking scrolls, *i i*, and *k k*, are fastened with clips ; the scrolls *k* are also secured to the cross B with solder or with clips ; *l l* are fastened to *k k* with clips, and to B with solder or clips.

On the scroll, A (Fig. 87), midway between the twisted portions, *a* and *a'*, the ornament, *m*, is fastened. Four, six, or eight of these small scrolls may be arranged at equal distances around the bar, A.

The actual candle holder is made and fitted into the hole made at c (Fig. 87). Figs. 92 and 93 show this fitting enlarged in section and in plan. A turned brass pillaret, n (Fig. 92), is riveted to A (Fig. 87) at c, and above to the dish, o. This dish is of thin sheet-iron of a conventional floral shape, and beaten up into a dished or concave form. Upon this the actual holder, p, of tin or brass tubing, is soft soldered.

A candlestick suitable for standing upon a reading-table is shown by Fig. 94. The centre-pillar, a, is of rod $\frac{1}{4}$ in. square, and four sets of scroll-work stand at right angles to each other; three sets on a triangular centre-pillar would serve as well and give less labour. The candlestick is from 10 in. to 14 in. high, and should be drawn out full size before beginning the work.

Beginning at the base, two double scrolls, b, c, $\frac{3}{8}$ in. or $\frac{1}{2}$ in. wide, and preferably $\frac{1}{16}$ in. thick, are turned and crossed at right angles. A hole of $\frac{1}{8}$ in. or $\frac{3}{16}$ in. diameter is punched in the centre of each, and the bottom end of the pillar, a, is shouldered into it and riveted over, as in Fig. 95. All the rest of the work is of thin iron. Three main scrolls, d, e, f, are in each series, as also the minor scrolls, g, h, j, k, and the tendril, l. These parts are shown separately by Fig. 96, in which the positions of the clips are indicated by single crosses. Double crosses show where the curves are clamped to the central rod and base. The tendrils, l, are fastened only at m, being clamped between d and e. Beyond that, they simply lie around the curves of d.

The dish, n (Fig. 94), of the candle holder is cut from thin sheet-iron, and is fastened to the rod, a, by a rivet passing through a hole in its centre. The candle socket, o, made of tin or brass tube, is soldered to n. The letters in Figs. 94 and 96 agree.

Fig. 97 illustrates a candlestick of an alternative design, but of the same general type as the last. As before, there is a central bar, *a*, riveted at bottom to the scrolled feet, *c*, and at the top to the dish, *n*, which holds the candle socket, *o*.

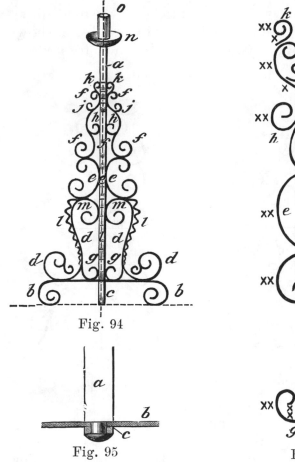

Fig. 94

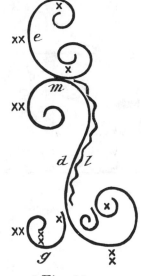

Fig. 95

Fig. 96

Fig. 94.—Table Candlestick; Fig. 95.—Base and Pillar of Candlestick; Fig. 96.—Scrolls of Candlestick.

The feet, *c*, should be of stout section, the remainder of thin strips. The scrolls, *d, e, f, g*, are clipped at their points of contact with each other, and also to the central pillar, *a*; and *b b* are minor scrolls.

Fig. 98 shows another alternative design, constructed similarly to the previous ones, but with different scroll-work. The various scrolls in a single series are shown separate by Fig. 99, and the previous remarks on fastenings also apply to this example.

The socket, *a*, of the candlestick, formed differently from those in the previous examples, is shown in detail by Figs. 100 and 101. It is cut from sheet-

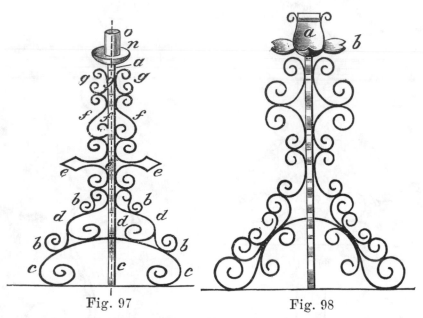

Fig. 97   Fig. 98

Figs. 97 and 98.—Table Candlesticks.

metal to the shape shown by Fig. 100; *a* is the sheet, shown again in Fig. 101, and seen also at *a* (Fig. 98), to be bent upwards on the four sides, and curled back again slightly at the top. This is soldered on to the rosette, *b*, also formed of sheet-metal, and riveted to the central pillar of the candlestick. The head of the rivet is shown at *c* in Fig. 101.

The last example to be shown in this chapter is the bedroom candlestick (Fig. 102). This has a handle *b*, but no central pillar, three legs, *a*, providing the necessary support (see also Fig. 103). The legs should be made of iron strips, $\frac{1}{16}$ in. thick, and the remaining curves of the thin strips. The

Fig. 100

Fig. 101

Fig. 99

Fig. 99.—Scrollwork of Table Candlestick; Figs. 100 and 101.—Forming Socket of Candlestick.

legs are prevented from spreading, and kept steady by means of a top ring, and two rings of double curves. The lower series, *c*, is shown in the plan (Fig. 103). These curves are united to each other with clips, and to the legs with the wire. Fig. 104

shows the details of the leg that carries the handle, *b*, the letters in this figure having the same references as those in Fig. 102.

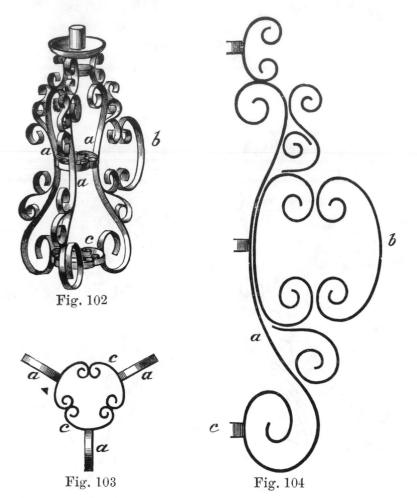

Fig. 102

Fig. 103   Fig. 104

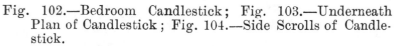

Fig. 102.—Bedroom Candlestick; Fig. 103.—Underneath Plan of Candlestick; Fig. 104.—Side Scrolls of Candlestick.

CHAPTER VI.

HALL LANTERNS.

LANTERNS are articles that can be very prettily constructed in bent iron. They admit of many and varied designs, and their mode of suspension gives scope for much ornamentation.

The lantern shown by Fig. 105 is of iron, brass, and copper, a highly effective combination. The main portions are of flat ribbon or hoop iron, the lamp-tray is sheet brass, and the trefoil ornaments are of copper.

For the iron-work 20 ft. of good quality ribbon iron, $\frac{1}{2}$ in. by $\frac{3}{32}$ in. (or No. 14 B.W.G.), with round edges, will be required. For the lamp-tray get a piece of No. 22 B.W.G. sheet brass 19 in. by $1\frac{1}{2}$ in., and another piece of the same thickness sufficiently large to form a disc, say, $6\frac{1}{4}$ in. diameter. For the ornaments get sufficient sheet copper of No. 22 or No. 24 B.W.G., for eight discs 2 in. in diameter, or, say, a piece 8 in. by 4 in. Twelve ball bolts of the size shown at Fig. 106 and twelve of a size smaller will be used, but it will be well to have more than the actual number required.

The bent iron side pieces first claim attention. Cut four lengths of the ribbon iron, each 3 ft. 6 in. long, for the sides of the lantern, and having an exact full-size working drawing of C, A, D, B (Fig. 105), upon some suitable surface, such as a large roofing slate, with which hard chalk can be used, the work of bending the scrolls, etc., may be begun.

Much of this bending is of necessity done hot, not cold. A good clear fire and a strong pair of

Fig. 105.—Hall
Lantern.

pliers are necessary. In the fire heat about 5 in. or 6 in. red-hot, and be careful not to exceed a good bright red, or the iron may be burned and spoiled. Grasp the extreme end of the iron in the pliers and form the small innermost turn of the spiral; then, by gradual bending, work the iron to the required shape—applying it from time to time to the working drawing—until the point A, Fig. 105, is reached. Chalk this point upon the iron, or if the metal is of good quality mark with a centre-punch. Heat to bright red as before, and double the iron as illustrated, so that the marked point may lie upon the centre of the bend. Screw up this bend in the vice very tightly, and if this is done quickly and dexterously the pointed portion of the scroll A (Fig. 105) will be formed. A

Fig. 106.—Ball Bolt.

little humouring of the iron, however, and perhaps re-heating, may be necessary.

The further shaping until the point B (Fig. 105) is reached, will be comparatively easy, and may be done cold, great care being taken to follow the working drawing exactly, as the whole success of the work depends upon this. To turn the point B (Fig. 105), repeat the operation as at A, and so on to the final scroll.

The other side pieces are now bent in the same way, applying each one to the drawing and also to that already made as the work progresses. In this way all four will be precisely the same both in size and shape, this being an essential.

The small scrolls in the angles (A, Fig. 105) are meant to give strength and rigidity to the sides.

For them, cut four lengths of iron, each 9 in. long. The spirals are turned in the same way as already described ; hold the iron with flat pliers in the left hand, while the shaping is carried on with the right. See that all four scrolls are

Fig. 107　　　　　　　　　Fig. 108

Figs. 107 and 108.—Rings of Hall Lantern.

exactly the same shape and that they agree with the drawing. Place them in position against the side pieces, and mark off the points of contact. Draw lines with a red pencil, etc., across the flat of the iron at each of these points, and mark decidedly in the centre with a centre-punch and hammer.

The drilling of the holes required for fixing the scrolls with the smaller $\frac{3}{16}$-in. ball bolts may be

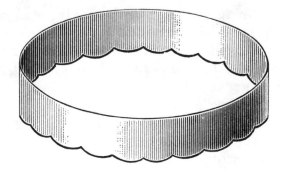

Fig. 109.—Lamp Tray.

done with any drill available, but the work is easier in a lathe. Insert the bolts from the inside of the small scrolls, and screw up nuts as tightly as possible on the outside ; cut off the bolts close to the balls, and rivet them by hammering, taking

Fig. 110.—Pattern for Lamp Tray.

care not to interfere with the shape of the side pieces, which during the fitting of the scrolls should be placed upon the working drawing.

For putting framework of lantern together, make two small hoops or rings, one 3 in. in diameter (Fig. 107) for the top, and the other 1¾ in. or 1½ in. diameter (Fig. 108) for the lower part of the lantern. For the former, it will be necessary to bend a piece of iron 10 in. long into a small hoop, scarfing and lapping ½ in. at the ends, which, if the worker is sufficiently skilled, may be welded ; or they may be neatly joined by a countersunk rivet. The other and smaller ring may be cut from a gun-barrel pipe of the required diameter, and should be about ¾ in. wide.

Having formed these rings, mark off four equi-distant points upon the centre of the outer circumference, and drill holes to suit the larger ball bolts in the larger ring, and for the smaller bolts in the ring of gun-barrel. Next drill corresponding holes in the side pieces at the points c and d (Fig. 105), or exactly at the points of contact with the rings when placed in position. Insert the respective bolts and screw up. Cut over-lengths and rivet as before directed, and the framework of the lantern will be complete.

The lamp-tray will be about 6 in. in diameter, and will be a hoop of sheet brass, 1½ in. wide, and scalloped on the lower edge (see Fig. 109). The exact diameter of the tray must be ascertained by correct measurement of the distance

between opposite side pieces, but assuming it to be
6 in., cut the strip of brass 19 in. long and 1½ in. wide ;
with a pair of compasses mark out the scallops
as shown in Fig. 110, and cut carefully with snips
afterwards, finishing the edges, sharp and regular,
with a fine file. To give a suitable finish to the
surface of the hoop, secure an old laundry iron,
face upwards, firmly in the vice, and using this as
an anvil, hold the hoop, right side up, flatly
upon it, and with the round end of a riveting
hammer go over the whole surface of the brass so
that the indentations shall touch each other, and
striking with uniform force and even distribution
of blows, a most effective mottled appearance will
be imparted. Bend the strip into a perfect hoop,
and having scarfed the ends with a file, lap them
for ½ in., and solder neatly, preventing any solder
from running upon the outside of the joint.

Cut out a disc of brass to fit tightly within the
hoop, and solder it in position about 1¼ in. from
the straight edge, or just above the scallops on the
lower edge. To do this, well clean the brass with
fine emery-cloth, apply killed spirit in the inside
angle of the tray, and using a very hot pointed
copper bit, cause a thin stream of solder to run
all round. If the parts of the tray have been
accurately fitted, a neat and strong job will be the
result.

The appearance of the tray will be much improved by dipping in an acid bath, and afterwards
lacquering. The dipping imparts lustre, and the
lacquering preserves it.

A good dipping bath for brasses is made with
1 quart of nitric acid, 1 pint of sulphuric acid,
and a pinch of common salt. Mix these in a glazed
earthenware vessel, and when cool (the mixing of
the acids evolves much heat) the bath is ready
for use. Wash the brass in a strong solution of
washing soda and hot water to remove all grease,

and using a hard nail-brush and finest ground pumice-stone, brush the whole surface of the brass, rinse in warm water, and allow to dry. Now run a piece of brass wire round the tray and across it, so that it may be firmly held, and having warmed it slightly, dip it completely into the acid bath; move it rapidly with a twisting motion for a few seconds only, and then rinse immediately and thoroughly in clean cold water. It should now be dried in a box containing hot box-wood or beech-wood sawdust, moving or shaking it about until all the moisture is absorbed. Do not handle it

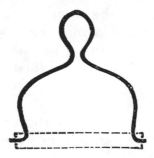

Fig. 111.—Hall Lantern Hanger.

without placing a piece of chamois or old silk handkerchief, etc., between the fingers and the brass. When all sawdust is brushed off the tray is ready for lacquering.

Eight trefoils have to be prepared as illustrated by Fig. 85, p. 48. Drill a $\frac{3}{16}$-in. hole in the centre of each, and then dip and lacquer them; use a colourless lacquer, if available, or the palest gold lacquer (see pp. 19 and 20).

The lamp-tray should now be placed in position, and holes drilled for its attachment to the four side pieces; fasten together with the larger-sized ball bolts, placing a trefoil upon each, as shown in Fig. 105. Attach the four upper copper orna-ments.

E

The hanger for the lantern may now be considered. F (Fig. 105) is of $\frac{1}{4}$ in. round rod-iron, and may be shaped as illustrated by Fig. 105, or as in Fig. 111. The legs must be exactly the same length and shape, and their ends are turned outwards at right angles, the bent part not being more than $\frac{1}{4}$ in. or so long. These are meant to pass through two holes, which should be drilled exactly opposite each other in the upper ring.

If accurately made and fitted there will be sufficient spring to allow of the ends being inserted from the inside, when the lantern should hang true upon the pivoted bearings.

With regard to the suspension of the lantern, a very light iron chain may be used, or a number of suspension rods may be made to hook into each other. A suspension rod is illustrated in Fig. 105, and alternative designs are given by Figs. 112 and 113.

A much more elaborate lantern is shown by Figs. 114 and 115, p. 68; it has ornamental chains and attachments suspended from a bracket, formed mainly of scrolls and rosettes.

The suspension bracket (Fig. 114) has two main frames, A and B, made by bending strips of iron of $\frac{1}{2}$ in. by $\frac{1}{16}$ in., or $\frac{3}{8}$ in. by $\frac{1}{16}$ in. section, into a triangular form. The joints are made by lapping, or by scarfing and riveting, and the two frames are united with the double curves, a. These should be clipped at three points, b, b, b, to the frames, but need not be united to each other. These outer framings must be straight and free from winding. The two large circles, c and D, should be of the same heavy section as A and B, because a good deal of work has to be fastened to them, and they tie B together. They are curved to lines struck on a board, or to wooden discs turned of the correct diameter. The end joints should be scarfed, and riveted or brazed. The circles should be riveted to B and to each other. The smaller circles, E, F, G, H, J, are made of the ordinary thin strips $\frac{3}{8}$ in.

Fig. 112   Fig. 113

Figs. 112 and 113.—Alternative Designs for Suspension Rods.

wide, and their ends may be soft soldered. They need only be soft soldered to the other circles, or to B, or even fastened with the common clips.

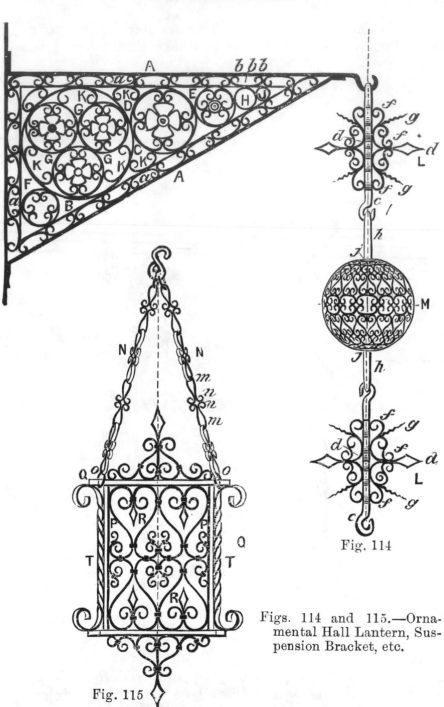

Fig. 114

Fig. 115

Figs. 114 and 115.—Ornamental Hall Lantern, Suspension Bracket, etc.

The centres of D and G are occupied with floral ornaments, fastened with double curves of bent iron to their respective circles. The flowers are cut from sheet copper, and hollowed out on a pitch block with a round-faced punch, and riveted in pairs back to back. The curves are clipped to the circles

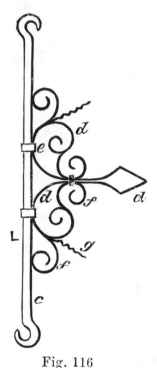

Fig. 116   Fig. 117

Fig. 116.—Detail of Suspension Star ; Fig. 117.—Segment of Suspension Ball.

which contain them and soldered to the edges of the flowers. Other curves, K, fill in open spaces.

Instead of suspending the lantern from a plain chain, there are several ornaments between it and the supporting bracket, the two star-like designs, L, L, and the ball, M, for instance. The stars are easily made. A central iron bar, c, $\frac{3}{16}$ in., or, at the most, $\frac{1}{4}$ in. square, carries the scroll-work. A hook is formed at each end of the bar by tapering down

and bending.   Each bar has four sets of scroll-work,
identical in design and size ; in plan they form a cross.
One set is shown by Fig. 116.   There is a main
double curve, *d*, with a finial, one on each flat of
the bar, *c*, and these are united to the bar and to
each other with clips at *e*, or with solder.   The minor
curves, *f*, are fastened to this with common clips.
Tendrils, *g*, are of thin iron bent backwards and
forwards with the round-nosed pliers ; they are
placed between their curves, *d* and *f*, and the clips
are made to enclose the three thicknesses.

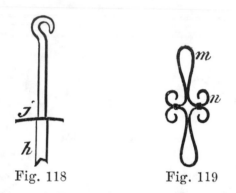

Fig. 118   Fig. 119

Fig. 118.—Part of Suspension Rod; Fig. 119.—Link for
Lantern Chains.

The ball, M (Fig. 114), is more difficult to make.
It is made of several built-up pieces, which in
general outline are like the surfaces of a segmented
orange (Fig. 117).   To make it, proceed as follows :
First prepare the centre-bar, *h* (Fig. 114), with hooks
at each end, just as in the case of the stars, or
large links, L.   At the positions, *j*, *j*, on the bar
corresponding with the diameter of the ball thin
circular discs are fastened by filing shallow shoulders
on the bar for the discs to abut against, and securing
them either with hard or soft solder (see detail,
Fig. 118).   The spherical curvature which is imparted to the discs will be the same as that of the
ball.   Prepare fourteen segments (Fig. 117), the

curves in which are clipped to each other at k, and to their fellows at each side at l (Fig. 117). The difficulty lies in imparting the spherical form. Each segment can be bent separately upon a template ball of wood. Then whilst uniting them into two separate hemispheres, each containing seven segments, use may be made of the same template, and gentle pressure of the hand will assist in obtaining the spherical form. The hemispheres are clipped together easily, so completing the ball.

The suspension chains, N (Fig. 115), for the lantern

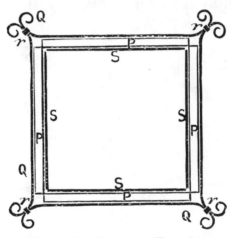

Fig. 120.—Lantern Framing.

are made of bent iron. Two links are shown in detail by Fig. 119. The links engage with one another at m, before the scrolls, n, are clipped together. The rings, o (Fig. 115) also are inserted before the adjoining curves are secured.

The lantern, o (Fig. 115), can be made in many ways. As illustrated the lantern is four-sided, but it may be triangular. It is glazed all over the sides, within the bent iron, but it may be glazed with oblong slips, or with circular discs only. There is no door, but it could have one if desired. The chains come down to the top of the lantern, but the corners of the lantern frame could be carried up in neat curves to meet the chains. The lantern has four frames, made of $\frac{3}{4}$ in. iron (see Figs. 115, 120, and 121). These may be of ordinary thin strips ; but it is better to take a length of $\frac{1}{8}$ in. square rod, heat it, and hammer it down until it is $\frac{1}{16}$ in. thick and $\frac{1}{4}$ in. wide ; this makes a substantial framing that can be worked without risk of distortion. Inside each frame, at top and bottom, and at a distance of $\frac{3}{8}$ in. along, a strip of thin iron, P, is fastened by turning down, and soldering in the ends. These strips receive the clips that attach the scroll-work at top and bottom, and the $\frac{3}{8}$ in. width is covered over by the strips, Q,

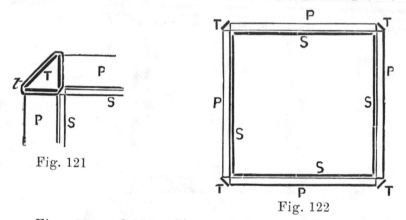

Fig. 121

Fig. 122

Figs. 121 and 122.—Glass and Corner of Lantern.

binding the frames, O, together. The frames are filled in with scroll-work, R, the main scrolls being fastened with clips to the frames and to each other also. The minor scrolls also are clipped in.

These frames can be united to each other in several ways. In the example illustrated by Fig. 115 the horizontal strips, Q (see also the detailed view, Fig. 120), act as binders, embracing the frames, being themselves held at the corners with clips, r. A little solder run between the faces at P prevents the parts from moving. The horizontal strips must be secured to the frames with clips or with fine wire, the former being preferable.

Some finish is required at the corners formed by the meeting of the frames; in Fig. 115 it is simply a double-ended scroll, T, of ¼ in. iron, with its rod twisted with the pliers. In Figs. 121 and 122 the scroll, T, is shown in the section of the thin iron near top and bottom, where it is fastened to P, P, with clips, *t* (Fig. 121). A little ornamentation at top and bottom completes the lantern framing. The scrolls at top and bottom are in harmony with those in the panels, and are fastened with clips similarly to the others.

Oblong plates of coloured glass, S, are placed

Fig. 123

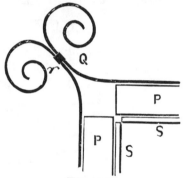

Fig. 124

Fig. 123.—Securing Glass to Lantern Frame; Fig. 124.—
Corner of Lantern.

within the lantern frames. They are secured with clips, as shown in Fig. 123, the ends, S, being turned down carefully after the insertion of the glass slips. Two clips at top and two at bottom are sufficient to hold the glass securely. In Fig. 124 the relative positions of these several parts are clearly seen, the outer frames, P, the horizontal binders, Q, and the glass, S. These parts are, of course, in contact, though in the illustrations they are shown separated a little to make the division between the parts quite clear.

The bottom of the lantern should properly be cut to fit within the frames, P (see Fig. 125, which is

a plan of the bottom). It rests on the inside of the
bottom bars of the frames, and may be of thin iron,
brass, tin, zinc, or copper. Fastening is not necessary, but it must be inserted before the frames are
secured to the top and bottom horizontals, Q. Upon
it may be soldered a candle socket, u, or a small oil
lamp may be stood upon it. This completes the
lantern.

Another design for a lantern is shown by Figs.
126 and 127, and an alternative method of making
the framing is shown by Figs. 128 and 129. Two
rectangular frames, A, A, are made with flattened
corners, and on the edges of these are soldered two

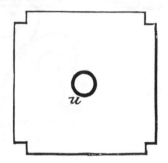

Fig. 125.—Bottom of Lantern.

other frames, B, B, so forming an angle-iron section.
Four corner strips, C, are bent round into double
scrolls, as shown, and these are riveted to A, A, at b.
Upper and lower scroll-work, D, E, is formed, and
also twisted shafts, F. C, D, and F are riveted at c.
D and a portion of C and F are shown in detail by
Fig. 128. Above there is a circular plate, G, with
ring attachment riveted into it. The plate is riveted
to D. The lower scrolls, E, are riveted to C and F,
and are themselves connected at the bottom with a
ring, J, riveted to them. This completes the main
framing. Thin bent iron will do very well for it,
the parts being well tied together, unless the lantern
is large, in which case iron about $\frac{1}{16}$ in. thick should
be used.

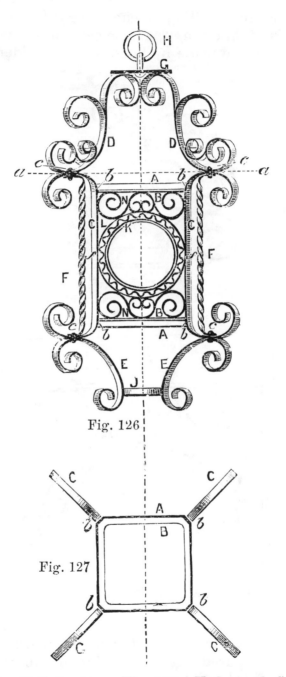

Fig. 126.—Hall Lantern ; Fig. 127.—Underneath Scrolls of
Hall Lantern.

The centre panelling on each face is formed thus. Two rings of thin iron, K, L (also seen partly enlarged in Fig. 129), are made by bending, and soldering or

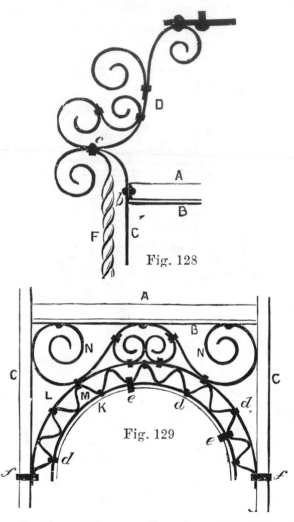

Fig. 128.—Portion of Lantern Framing; Fig. 129.—Lantern Panelling.

brazing. Between these a zigzag pattern, M, is fitted, and secured with clips, *d* (one clip at every second or third point of contact of the zigzag with the rings). Within K a disc of coloured glass is inserted, and held with clips, e, bent round as shown, and simply pressed against the opposite faces of the glass. The ring L is fastened to C, C with clips at f, f, and also to the scroll-work, N, as shown in the detail view, Fig. 129.

CHAPTER VII.

SCREENS, GRILLES, ETC.

THE screen shown by Figs. 130 and 131 may be used either as a fire-screen, or as an ornament merely. Its height may be from 2 ft. 6 in. to 4 ft. 6in., and other dimensions in proportion. Draw it out full size before starting to make it. There is some heavy work in the framing, but the whole of the tracery is formed of the thin strips of iron.

The framing is of iron bar, having a section of $\frac{3}{8}$ in. by $\frac{1}{16}$ in., or $\frac{1}{2}$ in. by $\frac{1}{16}$ in. The inner and outer frames, A and B, are connected with the scroll work, C.

The inner framing, A (Figs. 130 and 131), may be made of one strip, or more. If short lengths of iron only are available, joints may be made at the corners, or at any positions that may be convenient, by the method shown in Fig. 132, turning down the ends and riveting them to the verticals. A strip enough for the purpose, however, may be bent round at three corners and riveted at the fourth, in the fashion also shown in Fig. 132 ; or it may be bent round at all four corners and riveted in the centre of a length, as in Fig. 133, the joint being of the scarfed form; this latter is the neatest method. Or the joint may be lapped merely, and riveted as in Fig. 134 ; this, however, is not neat. The corners to be bent are well hammered over the sharp edge of an anvil or of a block of metal.

The outer frame, B (Figs. 130 and 131), is made in separate pieces. The top and sides of the frame, perhaps, might be bent round in one piece and fitted

Fig. 130   Fig. 131

Fig· 132   Fig. 133

Figs. 130 and 131.—Side and Front Elevations of Screen
Figs. 132 and 133.—Methods of Riveting Framing.

into the horizontal, B (Fig. 131), with a half-lap joint (Fig. 134), and if solder were run round, and

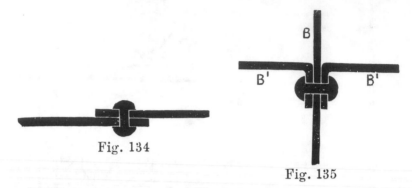

Fig. 134

Fig. 135

Figs. 134 and 135.—Methods of Riveting Framing.

the adjoining scroll brackets well secured, the frame would be firm. But the better plan is to fit the bar, B', in three lengths to the verticals, B, with turned-

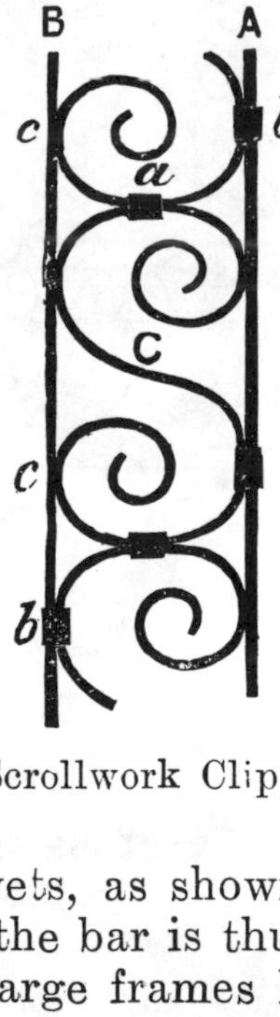

Fig. 136.—Scrollwork Clipped together.

down ends and rivets, as shown in Fig. 135. The entire strength of the bar is thus preserved.

When putting large frames like these together, hammer the bars quite straight in the directions of both width and thickness, and take care that the frames are free from winding when riveted together.

The two frames are united by means of the scrolls, c (Fig. 131), made of iron $\frac{3}{8}$ in. wide. These scrolls are arranged symmetrically on each side of the centre line, x—x, and one should be made first and tried between the frames, and when corrected, all the others should be tested with that one as a pattern.

When fixing scroll work, security is assured by as many clips (shown in detail by Fig. 136) as the parts will conveniently take. The scrolls are united

Fig. 137   Fig. 138

Fig. 137.—Construction of Scroll ; Fig. 138 —Scrollwork of Feet of Screen.

to each other at their ends, a (Fig. 136), and to the verticals A and B at two points, b, b. They could, of course, be also fastened at c, c, but this is unnecessary, as the clips are sufficient.

The scrolls D, E (Figs. 130 and 131) support the weight of the screen, and they, therefore, must be of the same section as the verticals, or about $\frac{1}{2}$ in. by $\frac{1}{16}$ in. The scrolls F and G may be of the same strong section, and will be riveted, and not clamped to the verticals, B, and to the horizontal, B′, at d d the rivets being of the snapped form, as shown, or else countersunk. These scrolls cannot be bent

F

with pliers, but must be hammered over the anvil-beak, either while cold or at a red heat. Try each upon the drawing, and upon its fellow, for symmetry.

The scrolls are formed of more than one piece, as seen in the detailed view (Fig. 137), where the parts are shown slightly separated to be easily distinguished. Thus, *e e* are formed of separate pieces, and fastened to D, either by soft or hard soldering, and the joint can be scarfed to make the scrolls appear as if worked from one piece. The tendrils at *f* are made, again, of separate strips, and inserted and brazed between the two scrolls, all being held together with solder.

The feet, E (Figs. 130 and 131) stand out sideways, and give steadiness. These are made of the same heavy section as the framing, and are riveted together at the bottom curve, *g* (Fig. 130), and are united at the top curve at *h*, to B, with stout clips or with spelter. In these, E is the main curve, to which the smaller, merely ornamental, curves are fastened with clips or with solder. These parts are shown separated in Fig. 138.

The broken scrolls, G (Fig. 131), are preferably of heavy section strips, say $\frac{1}{2}$ in. by $\frac{1}{16}$ in. These will be riveted at *d'*, at the end, a single rivet passing through D, G, and B. The minor scrolls, *e*, and the tendrils, *f'*, are soldered or brazed, as in the case of those on the opposite side of B.

The centre, H, of the bottom portion is a flower, or rosette, made of copper. In this example there are two such, placed back to back, fastened to each other with the rivet, *l*, that also forms the centre boss or disc. These flowers are cut from sheet copper of thin gauge, and after the dentations are formed by filing, the surface is hollowed with a round-faced punch upon a block of pitch. The iron circle, *m*, enclosing the flower, is soldered or riveted to the scrolls, G.

The panel of the screen is tastefully relieved by the coloured glass discs, K (Fig. 131). As the scroll work covers a large area, there must be a clip at every point of contact. The main curves, g, connect the inner frame A with the ellipse, J, and also partly support the frames that enclose four of the glass discs. The curves above the line, Y Y, are not symmetrical with those below, because the ellipse is placed above the middle line of the panel; but all the corresponding curves to right and left of the vertical line, x—x (Fig. 131), are symmetrical, so that, when one set has been

Fig. 139.—Part of Scrollwork Filling.

worked, the corresponding set can be tried upon them. All the minor curves, h, are fastened to the main ones with ordinary clips. The clips are not shown in Fig. 131, but Fig. 139 is a detailed view of the corresponding parts, J J (Fig. 131); in Fig. 139 the several scrolls, h, are separated, and the positions of the clips are indicated by crosses. The curves enclosed by the ellipse, J, are secured with clips, both to one another and to the ellipse.

The glass discs, K, may be held in position in either one of two ways. By the first method, a strip of thin iron, a, Fig. 140, is bent into an angular section, turned into a circle, and soldered at the ends (see Fig. 140). Then the disc of glass, *b*, can be laid upon the horizontal flange, and the top edge of *a* burnished or turned over by pressure, to cover and enclose the edge of the glass, as shown at the top of Fig. 140.

The second method of securing the glass discs is shown in Fig. 131. Make a true ring, *n*, of the

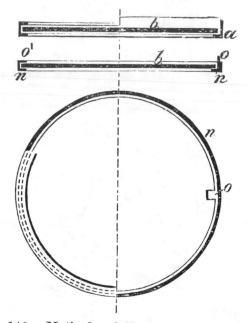

Fig. 140.—Methods of Fastening Glass Disc.

ordinary iron strips, and solder three or four short strips *o* (Fig. 140), to the outside of the rings equidistantly. Next unite the rings at their points of contact with the scrolls by means of the ordinary clips. Then the glass discs, *b*, may be slipped in, and the free ends of the short strips, *o*, are turned over against the face of the glass, as at *o'*.

The ornament, M (Fig. 131) at the top of the screen is made of the thin $\frac{3}{8}$ in. strips, and bent, and held with clips similarly to the other scroll work.

The grilles of mediæval times are especially

interesting and instructive to the smith and art
metal worker, as they exhibit generally a variety
of design in the scroll work, and a well-considered
construction showing considerable skill in the
manipulation of the material and its adaptation to
the purposes required.

The later Norman period of architecture in all
probability witnessed the introduction of grilles
and screens into the cathedrals and abbeys of

Fig. 141.—Grille at Winchester Cathedral.

England.   The same or similar designs appear to
have been in use in France and Spain at this
period.   The oldest remaining in this country is at
Winchester Cathedral, where it is now fixed against
the north door of the nave.   This will date probably
to about 1093.   Fig. 141 shows a portion of this
work.   The design consists of two rows of scrolls
welded to a central stem, the intervals between
being filled up with lesser scrolls.   The large
scrolls are about 5 in. in diameter, and are of stout

iron; this gives the whole grille great resisting power. The alternate scrolls are C-shaped, and at the junction of the back portion of the scroll are fixed to the stem with a wrought iron band. The

Fig. 142

Fig. 143

Fig. 145

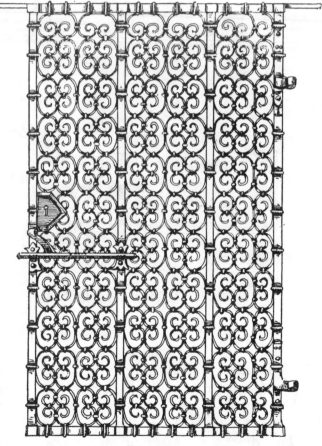

Fig. 144

Figs. 142 and 143.—Grille Terminals; Fig. 144.—Grille at Lincoln Cathedral; Fig. 145.—Scroll of Grille.

ends of the scroll are varied, some being forged into a trefoil (see Fig. 142); in these the end of the scroll is forged out, and the two smaller scrolls are welded on with a band at the junction. The other terminations are forged into a cinquefoil cluster, having the band in the centre (see Fig. 143). The heavy effect of the number of scrolls meeting at the central stem is obviated by thinning down the ends of the scrolls and welding them together. The scrolls are all fixed to the outer bars and rails with iron bands affixed to the bars with rivets. A similar grille is in the cathedral of Puy-en-Velay, France, which Viollet-le-Duc, the eminent architect, considers to be of a little later date than this one.

The grille from the cathedral of Lincoln (see Fig. 144) is an example of another class. It is constructed of strong iron bars riveted together, and filled in with simple C scrolls in couples, and is fastened together face to face with four band collars, and back to back with single collars. The enlarged sketch (Fig. 145) shows the method of fastening the scrolls together, and also of fixing them to the same work by means of an iron band fastened round the iron bars. As the choir and eastern transept of this cathedral were finished about 1200, and as it was necessary there should be a division between them from the beginning, it is probable the grille was made for this purpose. At this time it was probably surmounted by a cresting of spikes of some form, but these have disappeared.

The grille of Chichester Cathedral belongs to a rather different class of work, and of it, unfortunately, only a fragment remains. It is very diversified in its design, and has little symmetrical arrangement in it, thus being one of the most interesting pieces of work surviving. A portion of this work has been restored and re-erected in the cathedral. The grille illustrated by Fig. 146 con-

sists of upright bars riveted to the top and bottom
rails, the spaces being filled in with scrolls. The
great peculiarity of the work consists in the fact
that the design of the scroll changes at every
few feet very irregularly. Fig. 146 gives three
variations of scrolls, and the enlarged illustrations
of other portions of the grille (Figs. 147 and 148)

Fig. 146.—Grille at Chichester Cathedral.

show two other variations of the scroll work.
Many of the scrolls terminate in a stamped kind of
rosette, which, though of rude workmanship, shows
the commencement of the more ornamental work
which succeeded.

Fig. 149 gives an illustration of the more ornamental workmanship of a later date, the grille to
the tomb of Queen Eleanor in Westminster Abbey.
This work shows a distinct advance in making a

grille which was designed to protect something.
The object is accomplished by arching over the bars
forming the framework, and fixing on the top rail
a series of trident spikes, with the outer spikes

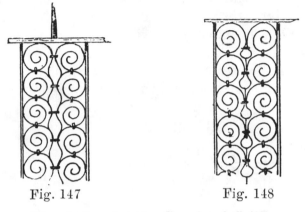

Fig. 147   Fig. 148

Figs. 147 and 148.—Panels of Grille.

sharply pointed and the centre ones arrow-headed.
This framework is of flat iron bars, on the face of

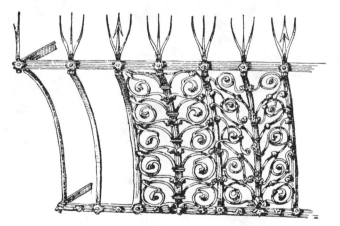

Fig. 149.—Eleanor Grille at Westminster Abbey.

which the ornamental panels are riveted. These
ornamental panels are of six different patterns, and
are similar to the hinge work of the period. This
work is flat as the hinges for doors, and is of beau-

tiful design and workmanship, the rosettes and
leaves and portions of the scroll work being
stamped in moulds when hot, thus showing a distinct advance in the ornamentation of ironwork for
this purpose, the commencement of which is shown
in the Chichester grille at Fig. 146. It is said that
this work was executed by Thomas of Leightone
in 1294.

The grille from St. Denis, which is a good
example of the later Gothic work, is shown by

Fig. 151

Fig. 150

Fig. 150.—Grille at St. Denis ; Fig. 151.—Scroll of Grille.

Fig. 150. The construction is similar to that of the
grilles before described, the scrolls being formed
of flat iron, and having the terminals hammered
out and cut into the shape of Gothic rosettes.
These scrolls are fastened to the constructive bars
with rivets. Fig. 151 is an enlarged illustration of
one of the scrolls, showing the leaf marking on the
upper rosette.

A portion of the iron grille of Santa Croce at
Florence is illustrated by Fig. 152. This is an
excellent sample of the quatrefoil grille panels of
Italy. In this the effects are produced by fitting
one bar of iron on another, and thus obtaining a

moulded effect. The circles are banded together
with collars, and the junctions of the quatrefoils
are curved and have pointed spikes. This is of
later date.

Fig. 153 is a sketch of one panel of a grille clos-

Fig. 152   Fig. 153

Fig. 152.—Grille at Santa Croce; Fig. 153.—Grille at
Freiburg Cathedral.

ing a chapel in Freiburg Cathedral, Germany; its
date is about the sixteenth century. It is dis-
tinctly Gothic in design, and well carried out.
The centre portion of the bars is thickened, and
left with the point of the square outwards. The
Gothic scroll work is of flat iron riveted together,

the terminations of the central bar and the base
panel being of hammered sheet iron.   The upper
finial is of pine-apple shape, of twisted round bars
on an open ball, with welded scrolls above.

These grilles exhibit a large and varied knowledge of the material used, and the best methods
of dealing with it, and are good examples of the
better methods of executing wrought-iron eccle-

Fig. 154.—Fireguard.

siastical and other work.   They are full of valuable
suggestion to the worker in bent iron.

The rest of this chapter will deal with work for
advanced workers.

A plainly constructed fire-guard or fire-screen
with open wire centre is shown by Fig. 154.   The
whole of the ironwork is fitted so that welding is
not required.   The foot is made of flat iron $1\frac{1}{8}$ in.
wide by $\frac{1}{4}$ in. thick (see Fig. 155), the longer portion
being bent into scroll form at each end (see Fig.

156); the short arms crossing are curved into C-scrolls. In these feet, at the point of junction, make a square hole by drilling a round hole, and making it square by filing. The end standards should be of iron ½ in. square, hammered to a

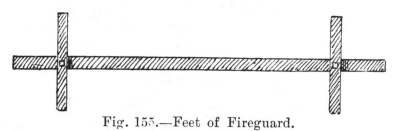

Fig. 155.—Feet of Fireguard.

round shape at the top and tapped to screw on the brass knob (see Fig. 157). At the bottom end (Fig. 156) make a similar tapped screw pin, and just above the screw file the square bar to fit the square holes in the feet and cross feet to the depth of the two bars, leaving a small edge for the standard to set down on.

The inner frame of the screen should be of

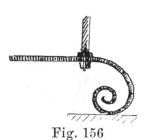

Fig. 156   Fig. 157

Fig. 156.—Scroll of Fireguard Feet; Fig. 157.—Top of Fireguard Standard.

round iron ⅜ in. diameter, to which the wirework may be fixed with wire twisted round the round bars. The small ornamental scroll at the top may be of flat iron ½ in. by $\frac{3}{16}$ in. This will make an artistic, but plain and useful guard. It may be improved in appearance by having an ornament, as shown in Fig. 158, of polished repoussé brass—that is, brass hammered up and then saw-pierced. This should be fixed in the centre of the wire work by small bolts and nuts. The iron work should be painted with Berlin black to dry dead.

A more ornamental fire-guard of shield form is illustrated by Fig. 159. The feet are constructed as before described. The side supporting standards are fitted into the square holes in the feet

Fig. 158.—Brass Ornament for Centre of Fireguard.

(see Fig. 160), this making a very secure fitting. Fig. 161 gives a section across the guard showing the construction. The side standards should be $\frac{5}{8}$ in. square iron, to which is fixed the shield centre of angle iron $\frac{5}{8}$ in. by $\frac{5}{8}$ in. ; and into this the centre woven wire, fixed on to a light frame, is put, being kept in place by round-headed screws to the feet and fastened in the centre with a small knob.

The spaces between the shield and the standards are filled in with wrought-iron scroll branches of ivy leaves and stems fixed to the bottom brace and side of shield with small screws. Figs. 162 and 163 give two alternative sketches for these leaves.

These ornamental leaf scrolls may, if desired, be in brass or polished copper.

The ornamental scroll above the top of the shield is affixed to the two standards at the end

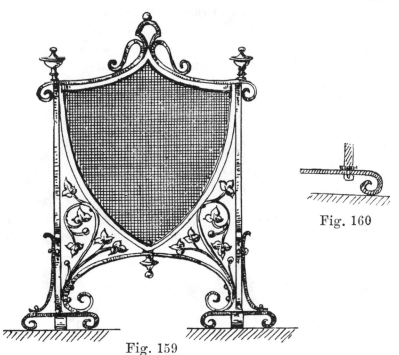

Fig. 160

Fig. 159

Fig. 159.—Fireguard; Fig. 160.—Foot of Fireguard.

by brass or copper knobs, which may be procured easily from any hardware establishment. If painted with a good quality Berlin black that will dry dead a very good effect will be gained. In similar

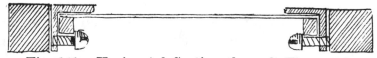

Fig. 161.—Horizontal Section through Fireguard.

fashion to the guard just described, a brass or copper ornament may be put in the centre of the shield, which will considerably heighten the general effect.

It is, of course, desirable that the fire-screen should correspond in character with the other accessories of the fireplace. Thus, if the fender and fire-irons are of brass, the fire-screen should be ornamented with brass. A very pretty effect would be produced by having all the furniture of the fireplace of iron and copper with a certain similarity of design. Fender stools and trivets are equally capable of artistic treatment.

A fire-screen may be made in various materials, such as iron with brass or copper mountings and

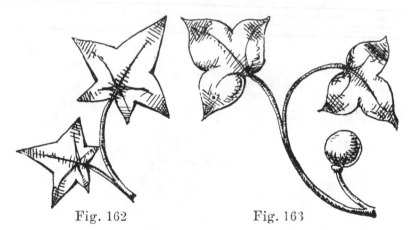

Fig. 162　　　　　　　　Fig. 163

Figs. 162 and 163.—Wrought-iron Scroll Branches and Leaves.

ornaments, or polished brass or copper with a metal plate, a mirror, plain or hand-painted, or a worked panel of plush or velvet. Fig. 164 shows a screen easily constructed. The square framework is of light angle iron, either welded or brazed (hard soldered) together at the corners. The supporting standards, as shown separate at Fig. 165, are of flat iron, 1 in. wide by $\frac{1}{4}$ in. thick, tapered at the top and screwed there to take a brass or copper ball. The feet are of the same size iron, turned up with scrolls as shown, and welded to the straight standard. The square frame is then fixed to the two standards with round-headed screws, as shown, and thus the construction is complete. The wide scroll feet enable the frame to stand upright.

The ornamental scrollwork round the frame is of flat iron, ½in. wide and ⅛in. thick. This can very easily be bent to the shape required, and with a little arrangement of the scroll ends welding need not be necessary.

Fig. 166 shows the method of fixing the metal

Fig. 164.—Fire-screen.

plate to the angle-iron frame. The plate having been cut to fit, the frame is secured by round-head bolts and nuts.

The pattern shown on Fig. 164 is arranged for repoussé work, which may be executed in copper, polished or antique, or polished brass. By working the plate in good copper, then rubbing it over with an oiled cloth and moving it over a gas jet

G

or fire, a variety of tints can be produced on the metal. It may then be lacquered to preserve the colour.

A design of a less ornamental character is shown by Fig. 167 ; it may be finished in any one of the ways suggested. The ironwork frame may be painted any colour to taste, but, to match with

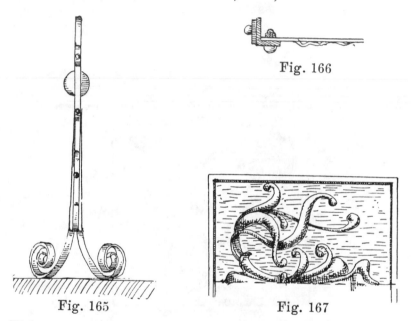

Fig. 166

Fig. 165   Fig. 167

Fig. 165.—Fire-screen Standard ; Fig. 166.—Fixing Copper Plate in Fire-screen ; Fig. 167.—Repoussé Copper Plate.

copper or antique copper, dead black will give the best results in appearance.

For the more elaborate screen (Fig. 168) a greater knowledge of iron manipulation is required. The standards (Fig. 169) are of $\frac{5}{8}$-in. round iron, turned over at the top, and with the double-scroll feet welded to the bottom, forming the stand for the frame. In the centre a number of wires are welded together at their ends and then to the upright of the standard ; they are then heated and twisted, forming the open ornament.

The standards carry the frame, which is of flat iron, ⅝ in. by ¼ in., fixed, as shown in Fig. 170, with a brass or copper ball and rosette; or, as shown in Fig. 171, with a brass or copper ornamental knob. The inner frame, of light ¾-in. angle iron, is octagonal, and is fixed to the outer frame with brass or copper spindles on the four square sides, as shown in Fig. 168. The corner spaces are

Fig. 168.—Fire-screen with Mirror Centre.

then fitted with wrought-iron leaves and scrolls, welded together. The ornamental top scroll-work is secured with round-headed screws to the top of the frame. A bevelled glass mirror, as shown in Fig. 168, is very effective in appearance, and is fixed, as indicated in Fig. 172, by a small moulding screwed to the angle-iron frame at the back.

Fig. 173 shows an alternative panel, which may be of brass or copper repoussé work and polished,

or made of antique copper, as before described,
or bronzed to any suitable colour. The fixing of
this metal plate is shown by Fig. 166, p. 98.

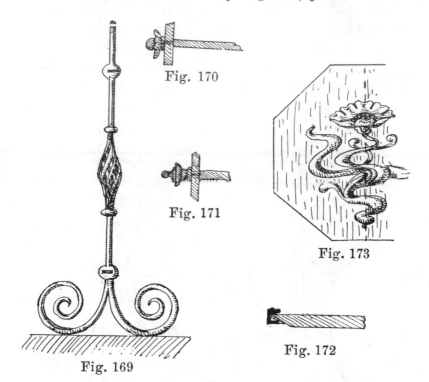

Fig. 170

Fig. 171

Fig. 173

Fig. 172

Fig. 169

Fig. 169.—Fire-screen Standard ; Figs. 170 and 171.—Fixing
   Fire-screen Frame ; Fig. 172.—Fixing Fire-screen
   Mirror ; Fig. 173.—Repoussé Brass Panel.

The colour of the ironwork may be left to the
taste of the maker, but, generally, dead black seems
to be the most suitable. Full information on finishing iron in bright and dead black is given on pp. 18
and 19.

CHAPTER VIII.

TABLE LAMPS.

THERE is scarcely a limit to the designs for table lamp supports in bent iron. Lamps with glass reservoirs can be used, but copper reservoirs are better, because with these there is no risk of cracking whilst mounting.

A simple mounting for a table lamp is shown by Fig. 174. A rim, a, goes round the bowl, and underneath this, and embracing the bowl closely, is a ring of thin iron, b, $\frac{3}{8}$ in. wide. This ring should be bent, and soldered or brazed, with ends lapping, say, for $\frac{3}{8}$ in. or $\frac{1}{2}$ in., and the joint neatly filed. To this ring the first scrolls, A, are wired, and there may be three or four sets of scroll-work, four being shown in Fig. 174.

The continuation of the scroll-work is in detail as follows: A short curve, B, fastened with a clip to A; a long curve, C, reaching from B to the foot D, and fastened to B and D; short curves, E, E, E, fastened with clips to C and to D. Two double curves, D, cross each other, and are riveted or soldered at the centre, where they cross. Small curves, F, F, may be added or omitted. The main series of curves being secured to the ring B above, and to the curves D, C below, the central part need only be stiffened with a ring at c, the curves being bound to it with wire.

A table lamp stand differently constructed is shown by Fig. 175. The lamp is taller, and the thin iron is supported with a central rod, a, of $\frac{5}{16}$ in. or $\frac{3}{8}$ in. square. To this four series of scroll-work are attached; the main scrolls are A, B, C, D, and there are also minor scrolls and tendrils. The rod *a* terminates at *b*, below; at the top it ends close beneath the bowl of the lamp. The bowl is enclosed with four scrolls, E, fastened with wire to the encircling ring, and riveted or soldered to the top end of the rod *a*.

The rest of this chapter is devoted to more

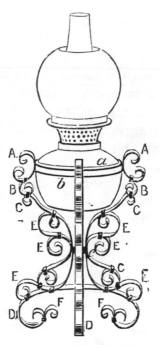

Fig. 174.—Table Lamp.

artistic and more difficult designs than the foregoing.

The bodies of the lamps may be in metal, clear glass, or opal. Clear glass gives the better effect in connection with the iron and brass or copper, unless a metal case is adopted, which then should be in whichever metal is adopted as the ornamenting metal.

The burner may have a frame of light brass wire, which could carry an ornamented shade of paper or silk with fringed edges; this softens the light and looks very artistic.

Fig. 176 gives the elevation of a lamp which

Fig. 175

Fig. 176

Figs. 175 and 176.—Table Lamps.

may be 16 in. or 18 in. high to the burner, according to requirements. The central pillar is of iron, $\frac{5}{8}$ in. square, twisted in the centre, shouldered and tapped top and bottom. The upper frame, which is to hold

the lamp body, as shown in elevation, Fig. 176, and
in plan, Fig. 177, is constructed of a ring of moulded
iron, or this may be flat, with the edges serrated,
supported on a frame of iron ½ in. by $\frac{3}{16}$ in. screwed
to the ring, and fastened to the central pillar by nut
and screw, fitting over a squared shoulder to give it
rigidity.

The ornamenting scrolls are fastened to the central pillar by round-headed screws.

The foot of the lamp stand is constructed of a
ring of moulded iron (see plan at Fig. 178, and section at Fig. 179) with an iron plate perforated orna-

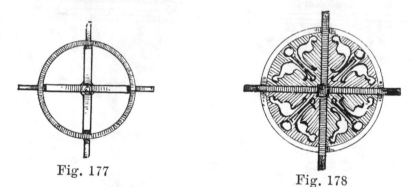

Fig. 177

Fig. 178

Fig. 177.—Top Framework of Table Lamp ; Fig. 178.—Base
of Table Lamp.

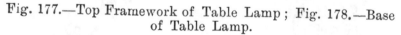

mentally, as shown, riveted on to the top of the ring.
The plate should be of ⅛ in. thick iron, or $\frac{1}{16}$ in. soft
steel. In the centre of this plate the central pillar
is fastened with nut and screw, as described for the
top frame. The scroll feet and supports (see Figs.
176 and 178) are of flat iron ½ in. by $\frac{3}{16}$ in. ; the feet,
of flat iron, are ⅝ in. by $\frac{3}{16}$ in., with the ends hammered out, formed into a scroll, and welded on to the
supports (see Fig. 178).

The leaves on the supports may be of sheet iron,
cut out and hammered up, and fixed by round-
headed screws or rivets to the supports. If these
leaves are made in brass or copper, polished and

lacquered, a much more artistic effect is produced. Fig. 180 gives an alternative design for the supports and feet, in which the leaves may be in brass or

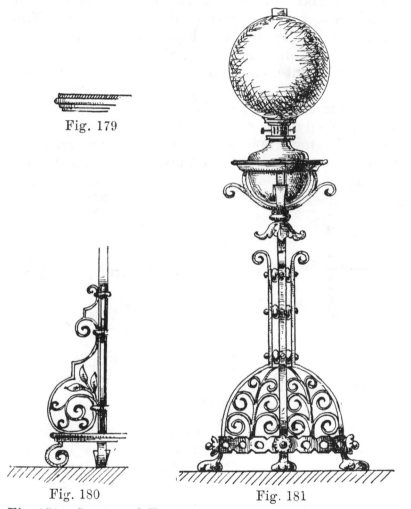

Fig. 179

Fig. 180   Fig. 181

Fig. 179.—Sect on of Table Lamp Base ; Fig. 180.—Alternative Design for Table Lamp Ornament ; Fig. 181.— Table Lamp.

copper. An equally good effect will be produced by having three supports and feet instead of four, as shown, and in this way the expense of making the stand will be lessened.

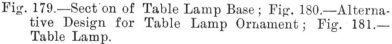

Fig. 181 gives the elevation of another design, the upper framework being constructed in the same way as before described, the leaf under the frame as shown in Figs. 181 and 182, being of hammered and chiselled metal, either iron, brass, or copper. The base of this standard (see Fig. 183) is formed by a ring of iron 1 in. wide by $\frac{1}{8}$ in. thick, with holes $\frac{1}{2}$ in. diameter at intervals and serrated on top and bottom edge between the holes. The four supports are of flat iron $\frac{5}{8}$ in. by $\frac{3}{16}$ in., bent as shown in Fig. 181, and fastened to the central pillar with round-headed screws having brass or copper flattened balls between them. The ends of these supports are ham-

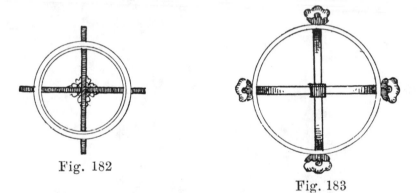

Fig. 182

Fig. 183

Fig. 182.—Top Framework of Table Lamp ; Fig. 183.—Base of Table Lamp.

mered up and upset and chiselled into the required form. The spaces between the supports are filled in with a tapered scroll stem fastened to the bottom ring and to the central pillar with screws. This tapered scroll is of $\frac{1}{4}$-in. round iron, tapered to the ends of the scrolls and hollowed to the shape of the supports so as to form a semi-globular shape. These tapered scrolls may be of brass or copper, but in that case the scrolls must be brazed together.

The ironwork of these lamps should be painted with dead Berlin black, or enamel of any colour may be used with equal effect.

CHAPTER IX.

SUSPENDED LAMPS AND FLOWER BOWLS.

A SUSPENSION lamp suitable for hanging in a passage or hall, either from a bracket or only from a hook secured to the ceiling, is illustrated by Fig. 184, the ornamental star from which the lamp hangs being shown by Fig. 185. The three suspension chains are formed wholly of ornamental links, but the lamp may be made for four chains if preferred.

With regard to the supporting link, beginning at the top, there is first the short hooked link A, Fig. 185. The central rod is $\frac{1}{4}$ in. or $\frac{5}{16}$ in. square, and the thin iron strips are of the same width as the rod, and the ends are tapered down and bent round as described at the end of this chapter (see Fig. 190, p. 111). The eight scrolls B, precisely alike, are fastened to A with clips. From the point of contact of the curves with each other the copper flowers C stand out upon their stems. The flowers are made as described on p. 44 and illustrated by Figs. 69 to 73.

To the rod, A, is attached the disc D, Fig. 184, from which the suspension chains depend. This disc is of sheet iron, or of copper of about 14 B.W. gauge ; its edges may be left circular and regular, or waved or toothed, and it is then dished by hammering. A ring a is riveted through a hole in its centre to receive the bottom hook of A. Three other rings are riveted at b to receive the eyes of the top links of the suspension chains.

The suspension chains E, Fig. 184, consist almost of a repetition of one pattern (Fig. 185), but smaller ; however, there is a slight variation in the curvature

Fig. 185

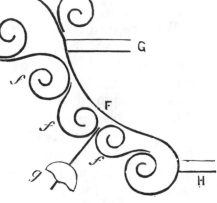

Fig. 186

Fig. 184.—Suspension Lamp;
Fig.   185. — Ornamental
Star for Suspending Lamp;
Fig. 186. — Scrollwork to
support Lamp Bowl.

Fig. 184

of the scrolls as illustrated. The central bar is not more than $\frac{3}{16}$ in. square, and does very well if $\frac{1}{8}$ in. square only. The thin iron strips must be of the same width. Four links are shown in each chain, but the number will depend upon the height from which the lamp has to be suspended. The eyes of the three bottom links pass through rings which embrace

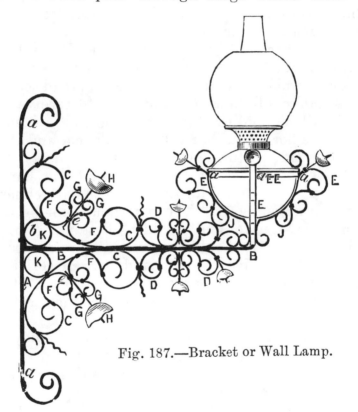

Fig. 187.—Bracket or Wall Lamp.

the scrolls F, Fig. 184, that carry the lamp. The bowl scroll-work is shown in detail by Fig. 186. There is a main scroll (F) and four minor scrolls (*f*, *f*, *f*, *f*). There is also a copper flower coming out at *g*, made as described on p. 44, and illustrated by Figs. 69 to 73. The scrolls are curved closely round the bowl of the lamp, and are united at top and bottom to the rings G and H. The ring G encircles the lamp bowl immediately beneath the beading *h*, Fig. 184; the lamp is, therefore, supported by the ring G. Diagonal wires unite the ring G to the scrolls F. The ring H beneath ties the scrolls together at the bottom, and is fastened with crossing wire.

The lamp has a chimney and shade, and the smoke glass shown above in Fig. 184.

A bracket or wall lamp is illustrated by Fig. 187. Almost any lamp may be used, but it is better to use one having a copper bowl.

For the back A, Fig. 187, get a piece of stout hoop iron of about 14 B.W. gauge ; taper off the edges at the ends, and bend them round to form broad scrolls. Drill and countersink holes at a, a, to receive the screws which hold the bracket to the wall. Square tenon the horizontal bar B into this back, and rivet over the end ; or turn one end of B upwards as at b, and rivet it to A. At the other end the bar is turned up for about 2 in. to receive the attachment of the lamp supports. The bar should not be less than $\frac{5}{16}$ in. square, and would be better if $\frac{3}{8}$ in. or $\frac{7}{16}$ in. square. It should be square, in preference to circular, to receive the top and bottom series of bent-iron curves, which stand opposite each other upon its two sides. The width of the thin strips is the same as that of the bar.

The main scrolls on the horizontal bar may be noted. On each of the two faces there are two main scrolls, C and D. A clip unites each series to B, and a rivet or solder unites C C to A.

The lamp bowl is united to the horizontal, B, in the following manner. Four strips of stout iron E, say, $\frac{3}{8}$ in. by $\frac{1}{16}$ in., are curved to fit the outline of the bowl, and prolonged to embrace the turned-up stem of B below, to which they are secured with two rivets passing through each pair of strips. At a the curves are wired to the encircling ring, E E, this completing the framework of main curves.

Taking the minor curves, those attached to C and D are of similar shape, but different size. The

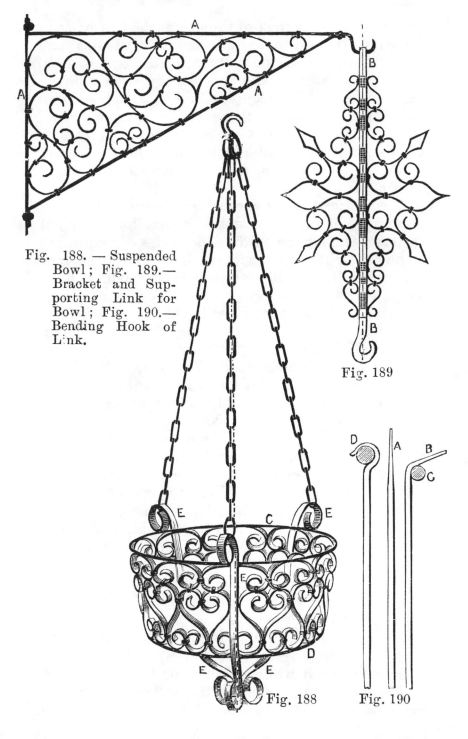

Fig. 188. — Suspended Bowl; Fig. 189.— Bracket and Supporting Link for Bowl; Fig. 190.— Bending Hook of Link.

Fig. 189

Fig. 188

Fig. 190

curves F, G are typical of those attached to D. F, F are each fastened to C at two points with clips, and to each other at e. G, G are also fastened to F, F, and to each other. The stem of the copper flower (H) is embraced between F, F and G, G, and secured with the clips that hold these scrolls together. Small circles are inserted at K, K, and tendrils at various places. The small supplementary curves J, J are wired to the curves D, and fastened to other parts with clips.

Two series only of curves are shown in Fig. 187, one above and one below bar B, but four or eight such series might be used. The series of four might stand at right angles with each other on the four sides of the bar, whilst series of eight would be fixed at angles of 45° with each other. Other modifications will suggest themselves to the reader.

A suspended vessel for ferns, flowers, grasses, etc., is illustrated by Fig. 188, its bracket and supporting link being shown by Fig. 189. The chains are of brass, and above is a star-like ornament. The chains are the only parts not made in bent iron.

Beginning with the bracket, Fig. 189, the outer framing A is made of bar, having a cross section of about $\frac{3}{8}$ in. by $\frac{1}{4}$ in. It is bent round and riveted, or brazed. The sides must be quite straight, and the frame free from winding. The large main curves are well clipped to the framing, and the smaller curves to both the main curves, and the framing. This is a very plain bracket. Others are illustrated by Figs. 67 and 114, pp. 41 and 68.

The supporting link, Fig. 189, has a central bar, B, of iron, about $\frac{3}{16}$ in. or $\frac{1}{4}$ in. square, tapered down at each end and turned round to form a hook. This operation is shown in detail by Fig. 190. At A, one end of the bar is seen tapered down. This is done by hammering it while red hot, or by grinding, or by filing. At B it is seen partly turned by hammering round the mandrel, C. At D the hook is seen completed round the mandrel. Upon each flat face of this bar a symmetrical arrangement of scroll-work is clipped. Seven separate pieces of iron are in each set, bent as shown, and clipped to each other. From the bottom hook of the star the three chains depend (see Fig. 188), and from these the ornamental bowl is suspended by the scrolls, E.

For the ornamental bowl, Fig. 188, two rings, C D, of ⅛-in. square iron are bent round and brazed with scarfed joints. The bottom ring is from 1½ in.

Fig. 191 —Bottom of Suspended Bowl.

to 2 in. smaller in diameter than the top one. To the rings C D the scrolls E are riveted, soldered, or wired, these scrolls being of stout iron, say ¼ in. by ⅛ in., or ⅜ in. by $\frac{1}{16}$ in. The ornamental bent iron around the bowl is formed of ten similar sections. These are prepared separately, and clipped to the rings C D, and to each other. The precise form of the curves is obtained by dividing the lengths, which are equal to the circumference of the circles C and D, each into ten equal parts ; and a middle imaginary circle midway between C and D, also into ten equal parts, when the lines drawn through these three points of division will be the bounding lines of the curves. Ten similar sections, bounded by these lines, will, when united, form the outline of the bowl.

H

The bottom of the bowl can be formed in various ways. The simplest is that shown by Fig. 191, in

Fig. 192.—Incandescent Gas Hall Lamp.

which a number of similar double or c curves are clipped to the bottom ring B, and to each other.

The frames for hanging lamps illustrated by Figs.

192 to 194 are designed to be made in bent iron, with copper or brass ornament fixed with copper bands and rivets.   It is advisable to procure the globe and

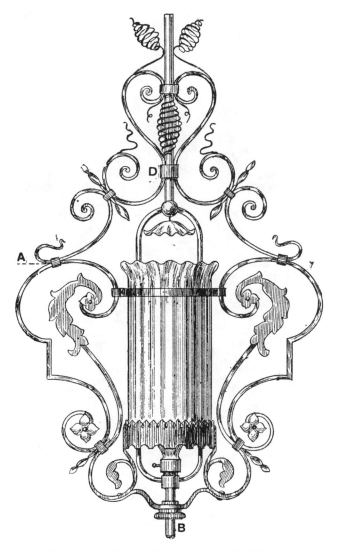

Fig. 193.—Incandescent Gas Hall Lamp.

burner before proceeding to make the frame.   The globe in Fig. 192 is 5 in. in diameter at the base and 9½ in. high, the extreme height of the frame being

2 ft. 1 in., and width 1 ft. 2 in.   The vertical distance
from the rings A to the nut B is 10½ in.   The glass
in Fig. 193 is 3¼ in. in diameter by 7½ in. high,

Fig. 194.—Oil Lamp for Hall.

the extreme height of the frame being 1 ft. 9 in., and
the width 12½ in., the vertical distance from A to B
being 11 in.   The height of the frame shown by

Fig. 194 is 1 ft. 8 in., the extreme width being 1 ft. 1 in., and the diameter of the reservoir 4 in.

Make a full-size drawing in single line of the prin-

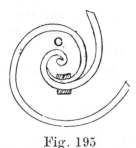

Fig. 195

Fig. 196

Figs. 195 and 196.—Scrolls of Hall Lamp.

cipal curves, one side only being drawn. The length of the curves may be found by bending copper wire round the scroll on the drawing, afterwards straightening it out; then cut off iron to the length of the wire, and from the drawing make templates of the

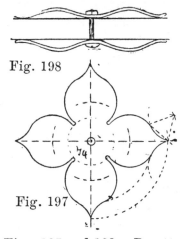

Fig. 198

Fig. 197

Figs. 197 and 198.—Rosette.

scrolls from $\frac{1}{8}$-in. round iron wire. These are used for reference when bending, and are especially useful should the scroll require heating. If the iron proves hard to bend, as it sometimes does when much hammered and bent while cold, it should be annealed by heating to redness in a fire and then burying it in ashes or lime till cool. The section of the iron may be $\frac{1}{8}$ in. or $\frac{3}{16}$ in. by $\frac{1}{2}$ in. or $\frac{5}{8}$ in.

Referring to the lamp shown by Fig. 192, before commencing to bend the scroll C, taper one end for the top, and first bend over $\frac{3}{8}$ in. as at C (Fig. 195). The scroll D (Fig. 192) has a leaf ornament, formed by giving the end, while hot, a half-twist, and hammering it out flat on the anvil. Fig. 196 shows the leaf; the shaded part should be cut and filed to shape. To the top part of this scroll are attached

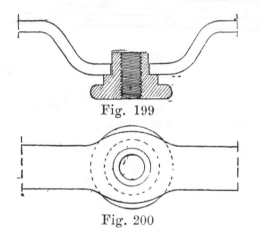

Fig. 199

Fig. 200

Figs. 199 and 200.—Milled Nut and Strap.

two small rosettes, one on either side, these being fixed by small bolts and nuts. There are eight rosettes on this frame; they should be made from very thin sheet metal. With dividers mark out one on thin tinplate (see Figs. 197 and 198), and cut carefully to the lines; use it as a template, holding it firmly with one hand on the sheet copper while scratching round it with the steel scriber. The leaves and tendrils which are not part of the scrolls are riveted through a small drilled hole.

The part of the framework carrying the globe is detachable for cleaning and renewal of mantles (see

Figs. 199 to 203), and is removed with the globe still attached by turning the split rings A (Figs. 192 and 193) in the position shown by Fig. 203, where the

Fig. 201   Fig. 202

Figs. 201 and 202.—Parts of Framework carrying Globe.

dotted lines show the part released. Next unscrew the milled nut B (Figs. 192 and 193) and the whole will come away. The rings should be notched or milled on the outside. Figs. 199 and 200 shows plan and section of a milled nut and strap, and by referring to Figs. 201 to 203 it will be seen that the section of the scrolls is wider than the inside diameter of split ring because the scrolls are filed as shown at Y (Fig. 202), to prevent lateral movement. This

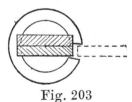

Fig. 203

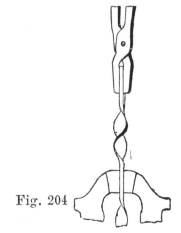

Fig. 204

Fig. 203.—Split Ring ; Fig. 204.—Making Twist Ornament.

arrangement will not be required for Fig. 194, as the reservoir will lift out when the chimney and globe are removed. Where two scrolls terminate at the same centre (see Fig. 195), the one that laps should be tapered as shown to prevent unsightliness. Fig. 204 shows the method of making twist ornament, while Fig. 205 shows a section of the copper rings D

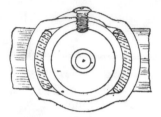

Fig. 205.—Section through Copper Rings.

(Figs. 192 and 193). The part of the scroll in contact with the pipe is hammered over to fit, and the ring is further secured by a set-screw through the lap. The ironwork should be painted dead black, and the copper ornament polished and lacquered.

CHAPTER X.

PHOTOGRAPH FRAMES.

A DOUBLE photograph in bent iron work to stand on a table is illustrated in front and side view by Figs. 206 and 207, pp. 122 and 123. The oblong frames to contain the photographs should be made of sheet iron bent to angle shape, and with one edge serrated. Into these frames the photographs are placed, with a piece of wood of the thickness of the iron angle behind, which wood is kept in place by screws, as shown at A, Fig. 206. The bent iron scrolls may be affixed together with wire or flat strap bound round or riveted. The frames containing the photographs should be screwed or riveted to the scrollwork. Where two or three scrolls come together at the end it will be well to rivet them, and then wrap the strap or wirework round.

To vary the work, the monograms and some of the minor scrolls may be in copper or brass ; this must be left to the taste of the worker. The supporting scrolls on which the frames stand should be of slightly thicker and wider iron, so as to give the appearance of stability, and also the extra strength required. If it is wished to make the photographs stand at a slight angle instead of upright, as shown, this may be done by reducing the height of the back leg, which will have the effect of throwing the frames back to the angle required. With a little thought, several designs may be produced from the sketch illustrated.

To supply the needs of advanced workers who are wanting photograph frames of designs superior to those usually made in bent iron, the illustrations (Figs. 208 to 210) are given, the actual work to be executed in iron. For work of this kind the best quality iron only should be used, as the weldings are small

Fig. 206.—Double Photograph Frame.

and fine, and need very great care in manipulation. It adds very greatly to the appearance of the work if portions are executed in brass or copper or aluminium, polished bright or dead. The bright colouring gives an excellent effect in connection with the black iron.

Fig. 208 is a complete frame for a single photograph, which is placed within a shield-like frame
of brass, copper, or aluminium.   This frame should
be slightly hollowed towards the front edge, so that
the glass may set down flat, the photograph and

Fig. 207.—Side Elevation of Photograph Frame.

glass being kept in place by a cross-plate fastened to
the back of the frame with screw nuts.   The
wrought-iron outside framework should be made of
iron $\frac{1}{4}$ in. or $\frac{5}{16}$ in. wide by $\frac{1}{8}$ in. thick, welded together in the position shown, and riveted in other
parts.   A pretty effect is produced if the ends of the

scrolls are hammered out wider before being bent to shape.

The leaves forming the central wreath should be cut out of best Swedish or charcoal sheet-iron, with a length of about ½ in. left at the end of each for

Fig. 208.—Single Photograph Frame.

welding on to the stem, which is of round iron about ⅛ in. diameter. The balls may be made by turning over the round iron and hammering into ball shape. Great care must be exercised in welding, one group of leaves with the accompanying berries being executed after another, so that they are not allowed to

get too hot and burn the iron.   These wreaths are
then fitted into the framework and fastened with
small rivets.   The brass or copper frame holding
the photograph is held on the face of the framework

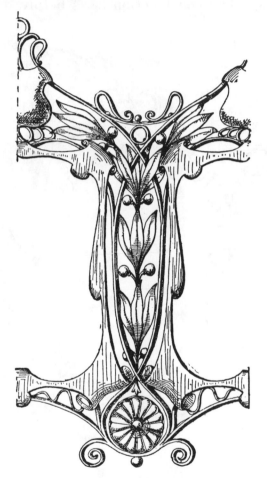

Fig. 209.—Part of Double Frame.

by screws and nuts passing through and fastening
at the back.

The shield at the top, which is intended for the
monogram or name of the portrait, is fixed with
screws and nuts in the same way, as are also the
two rosettes at the bottom of the framework.   The

ironwork should be painted a dull black, or any other dark, dead colour.

Fig. 209 shows the arrangement for the same photograph frame when required for two cabinet portraits. The construction is as before described,

Fig. 210.—Double Photograph Frame.

the necessary alteration being made in the central portion.

Fig. 210 shows a double frame of another design, having larger, bolder leaf-work and berries. A little care is required in the hammering up of the leaves, so as to get variety in effect. The frames holding the photographs are in this case made of angle sheet-iron, cut out to shape as shown, and with the ball hammered up from the back. These frames are fixed to the outer work, and form part of the completed frame. The photograph and glass fit in from the back, and are secured by screws or by an iron plate screwed on to the edges.

Single photograph frames may be made from the design (Fig. 210) by using the half-circular central ornament over the single frame, and repeating the top and bottom side scrolls.

CHAPTER XI.

NEWSPAPER RACK.

A RACK for newspapers, magazines, letters, etc., can be made in bent iron with two side panels connected by side brackets at the bottom, the panels being at an angle to give the greater width at the top (see Fig. 211).

The method of construction is shown in plan by

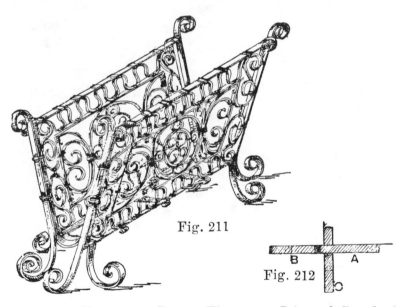

Fig. 211

Fig. 212

Fig. 211.—Newspaper Rack; Fig. 212.—Joint of Standard and Foot.

Fig. 212, in which A is the panel frame, B the supporting scroll leg, and C the double supporting foot. Fig. 213 shows the end standard support with a scroll at the top and foot, the outer frame of the side panel being fastened to it.

Fig. 214 shows the arrangement for jointing the outer frame of the panel. The strips are squared round the four sides, leaving the joint at the centre

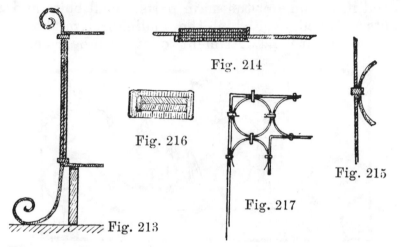

Fig. 214

Fig. 216

Fig. 215

Fig. 217

Fig. 213

Fig. 213.—Newspaper Rack Standard and Foot; Fig. 214.— Frame Joint; Figs. 215 to 217.—Scroll Fastening.

of the bottom. Each strip is left 1 in. longer than needed, and the end turned just to the thickness of the band. These ends being placed together, the

Fig. 218.—Newspaper Rack Panel.

band iron is hammered round them, making a firm joint. Figs. 215 to 217 illustrate the method of fixing the scrolls to each other and to the framing.

The two side panels are, say, 13 in. long by 8 in.

I

or 9 in. deep.   The outside frame is of iron, about
$\frac{5}{8}$ in. wide, the inner squared portions $\frac{1}{2}$ in. wide, and
the scrolls $\frac{3}{8}$ in. wide.   The rack will be strengthened if, at some of the main parts, small bolts and
nuts are fixed, over which the binding iron might be
placed, but it is no detriment to let them be seen.

Fig. 219

Fig. 220

Figs. 219 and 220.—Newspaper Rack Panels.

Fig. 218 gives a panel with the ornamental scrolls
round, and the date of the year worked in scroll iron,
while Fig. 219 shows a similar panel, but with the
word "news" worked in.   These designs may be
worked in polished copper or brass strip, and a
pretty effect is produced at very little extra cost.

Fig. 220 shows a panel in which the only ornamentation is scroll-work of brass or copper.

CHAPTER XII.

FLOOR LAMPS.

A SIMPLE floor or standard lamp in bent iron is shown by Fig. 221. The majority of these lamps have been made in forged iron or in brass, but bent iron is equally suitable. The ornamentation may either be wholly in bent iron or partly in iron of stout section and partly in thin strips, the latter system being preferable because it is stronger.

The central pillar, A, Fig. 221, must be stout, not less than $\frac{1}{2}$ in. square. It is riveted at the bottom to the two crossing curves B, B, made of iron $\frac{1}{2}$ in. by $\frac{1}{8}$ in. The curves C, C, made of stout iron of similar section, are riveted to A at a, a, and to B at b.

The upper work may be of thin iron wholly. The main scrolls D, E, F, G, are clipped firmly to the central pillar, A, the clips embracing at once the four corresponding scrolls lying against the four faces of the bar. Fig. 222 shows the way in which each series is built up, clips being employed as fastenings.

The lamp bowl, H (Fig. 221), is of copper, and has the usual beading, d. An iron ring e, fitted underneath and around this, supports the bowl; and the scrolls J, K, carry the ring, and are fastened at L to the pillar, A. This particular work may be of thin iron, but it is better to use stouter material, such as $\frac{1}{2}$ in. by $\frac{1}{16}$ in., or $\frac{3}{8}$ in. by $\frac{1}{16}$ in.; the lamp bowl will then be steadier than if carried by thin strips. A single series of these curves is shown in detail by Fig. 223. The two curves, J and K, are riveted or clipped together, but if there is difficulty in firmly uniting these, substitute one curve for the two. The principal point to

Fig. 221   Fig. 222

Fig. 221.—Floor Lamp ; Fig. 222.—Floor Lamp Scrolls.

be noted here is the union of the four curves, J, to the pillar, A. These curves are brought down a considerable distance below the end of A, say 2 in., so that they can be united with two rivets. Two rivets will pass through from side to side at, say, 1 in. or $1\frac{1}{4}$ in. centres, to hold the curves which come upon opposite faces, and two will pass through from the other sides at right angles with these at the same

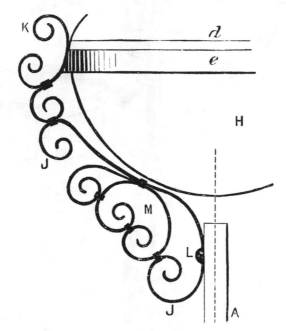

Fig. 223.—Scrolls at Lamp Bowl.

centres, but about $\frac{1}{4}$ in. above or below the others, to hold the remaining two curves. The long open space then is filled in with a small scroll, M.

The floor lamp shown by Fig. 224 is a specimen of heavy bent iron and forged work. It has a handsome appearance when completed with a large silk shade.

The materials required are a brass rod 4 ft. long and $1\frac{1}{2}$ in. in diameter, about 30 ft. or 40 ft. of the best iron (coachmakers' hoop-iron, some ironmongers call it), about 12 B.W.G., and either $\frac{3}{4}$ in.

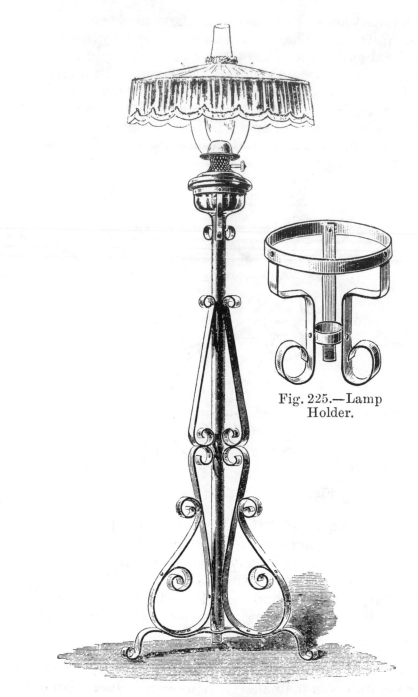

Fig. 225.—Lamp
Holder.

Fig. 224.—Floor Lamp.

or $\frac{1}{4}$ in. wide, or both widths can be used—the wide
for the bottom parts and the narrower for the top—
and two or three dozen bolts. The brass rod must
be free from blemishes ; the cased brass may be used
if it can be got the proper size, and it will be
cheaper.

Enlarge the designs to full size, and either draw
the pattern upon plate, or make the design in wire,
which is easily bent, and which will serve as a guide
when forming the first piece, the others being made

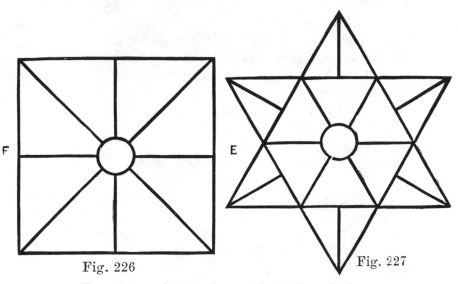

Fig. 226   Fig. 227

Figs. 226 and 227.—Lamp Shade Foundations.

to that. Three pieces of each pattern will be required. Care will be needed in bending, and a
better finish will be given if the bend is made by
pulling round something when the iron is hot rather
than by hammering or using pliers. When all the
bends are finished, drill the holes for the bolts or
screws ; if the latter are used, tap the holes and cut
off flush ; but with bolts it will look better to make
copper ornaments, as described in Chapter IV.
Fig. 225 shows the lamp-holder, one-quarter full
size.

Having given the stand two coats of drop-black,
fit together all the pieces, screwing the iron to the
brass rod, and putting a bolt through the three feet
where they unite underneath the rod.   The dots in
Fig. 224 show where the bolts go.

The shade is made of a foundation of wire soldered together, covered with silk and lace, and lined
inside.   It may be made any size from 15 in. to 24 in.,
and either round, square, or any fancy shape (see
Figs. 226 and 227).   Make the centre and the outside
first ; then, if the connecting wires are cut about 1 in.
longer than the measure when laid flat upon a table,
this will raise the centre to the proper height.

The standard lamps now to be treated have been
designed for easy construction in wrought iron, thus
giving the strength required, the ornamental portions being in bent ironwork.

The arrangement for the sliding upper portion of
the standard carrying the lamp is the same in all
the lamps illustrated by Figs. 228, 232, and 235.   A
brass turned boss or collar, into which is screwed a
brass tube $\frac{3}{4}$ in. in diameter, is fixed to the bottom of
the lamp.   The main tube may be of iron $\frac{3}{4}$ in. inside
diameter, with a turned brass or copper collar
screwed to it.   Through it slides the brass tube, this
being held in any required position by a set-screw
as shown in Figs. 228 and 232. The light frame of iron
or brass wire which supports the lace shade is also
fixed by means of screws to the upper collar under
the lamp.

Fig. 228 shows a standard lamp of simple construction, the tripod base being the only portion re-
quiring welding.   The iron for the base should be
$1\frac{1}{4}$ in. by $\frac{3}{8}$ in., welded together in the centre as
shown in Fig. 229.   Into this the iron central tube is
screwed and fastened by a hexagon nut.   The three
supporting scrolls should be of iron 1 in. by $\frac{5}{16}$ in.,
fastened to the tripod stand with nuts, and to the
upper end of the central tube by collars screwed to

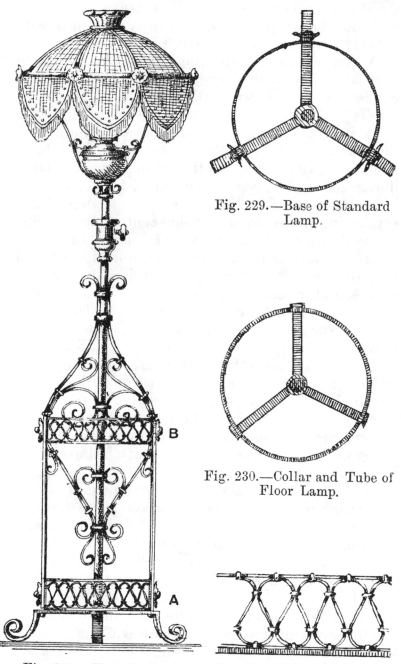

Fig. 229.—Base of Standard Lamp.

Fig. 230.—Collar and Tube of Floor Lamp.

Fig. 228.—Floor Lamp.

Fig. 231.—Ring Ornament.

the iron tube as in Fig. 230. Two ornamented rings
of bent iron are fastened to the scroll sides with
brass rosettes as shown by A B, Fig. 228.

A detailed view of the ring ornament is given by
Fig. 231. The central ornaments of bent iron are
clipped to the central pillar and the supporting
scrolls.

A standard lamp of triangular construction is
illustrated by Fig. 232, the upper parts of the lamp
and sliding tube being similar to those for the lamp
illustrated by Fig. 228. The tripod foot of iron, $1\frac{1}{4}$
in. by $\frac{3}{8}$ in., rises in the centre in triangular form,
say 12 in. from the floor, the central tube being
screwed to the welded centre (see Figs. 233 and 234).
From each arm of the tripod fix an iron side strip of
1-in. by $\frac{5}{16}$-in. iron, bent as shown in Fig. 232, and
secured to the central tube at the top by collars, and
at the bottom with small bolts and nuts. The spaces
between the central tube and the side stays are filled
in with ring patterns in bent ironwork and secured
with bent iron slips. The triangular foot or stand
is filled in with a pattern in bent ironwork fixed to
a triangle of $\frac{3}{4}$-in. by $\frac{1}{4}$-in. iron secured to the tripod
stand with a round head bolt and nut. The ring
pattern as shown may be made more ornamental by
filling in the ring with trefoil or quatrefoil ornament
in bent iron clipped to the ring.

A lamp of a much more ornamental character, so
far as the bent ironwork ornamentation is concerned,
is shown by Fig. 235. The lamp and sliding fittings
are similar to those before described. The tripod
foot with welded centre, into which the central tube
is screwed (Fig. 236), may be 10 in. or 11 in. from the
floor line, and is of $1\frac{1}{4}$-in. by $\frac{3}{8}$-in. iron with scroll
ends. A better effect is produced if the ends of the
scrolls are widened out by hammering when hot.
The side stays, of 1-in. by $\frac{5}{16}$-in. iron (Fig. 235), are
curved, and have scroll ends at the top fixed to the
central tube by collars and at the tripod foot with

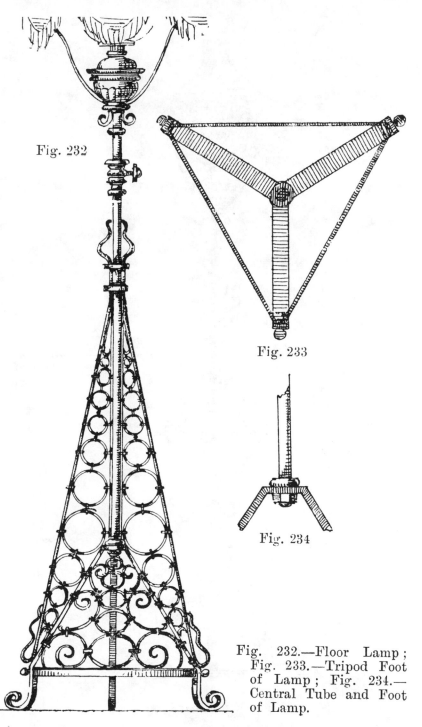

Fig. 232

Fig. 233

Fig. 234

Fig. 232.—Floor Lamp;
Fig. 233.—Tripod Foot
of Lamp; Fig. 234.—
Central Tube and Foot
of Lamp.

Fig. 235.—Floor Lamp

bolts and nuts. Fig. 237 shows the method of screwing the central tube to the tripod foot, and also of fastening the under stay support.

The bent iron ornamentation (Fig. 235) should be made in panels of the shape of the space between the side stays and the central tube, to which they are clipped in. This pattern may be simplified by

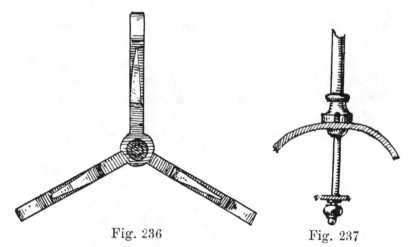

Fig. 236   Fig. 237

Figs. 236 and 237.—Tripod Foot of Lamp.

leaving out some of the central scrolls, and the small upper scrolls under the brass collar boss may also be omitted without detracting from the general appearance.

When finished these lamps should be painted a dead black; or a better effect would be produced by painting the constructional wrought-iron portions dead black and using polished brass or copper strips for the scroll-work ornamentation.

CHAPTER XIII.

MISCELLANEOUS EXAMPLES.

CANDLESTICKS are treated in Chapter V., but the sconces about to be described are an advance on any there illustrated. Candle sconces can be made up in iron or brass, or in a combination of iron and copper, and Figs. 238 and 239 are to be made of brass polished and lacquered. The metal may be $\frac{1}{16}$ in. or $\frac{3}{32}$ in. thick by $\frac{1}{2}$ in. wide ; the distance of the scroll

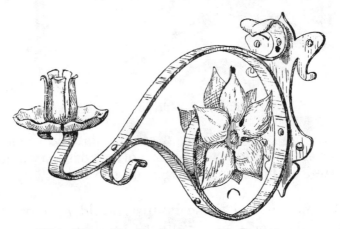

Fig. 238.—Candle Sconce with Rosettes.

from the fixing plate to the centre of the holder is 7 in., and the depth is 3½ in.

Figs. 240 and 241 are designs intended for bent iron, $\frac{1}{16}$ in. to ⅛ in. thick ; the latter is about the limit for bending cold. The back plate, candle-holder, and saucer can be made of copper, but the iron scrolls are painted generally dead black. The large scroll in Fig. 240 varies in width, and this variation may be allowed for in cutting out or be ob-

Fig. 239.—Candle Sconce with Rosettes.

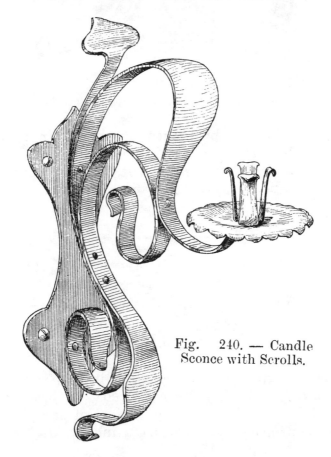

Fig. 240. — Candle Sconce with Scrolls.

tained by hammering while hot. Begin by making a wire template of the scroll, and straighten out the wire, when it will represent the length of material required. Procure the brass strips of the proper

Fig. 241.—Candle Sconce with Scrolls.

width, or the next best method is to obtain a length of brass banding used for lagging and $1\frac{1}{4}$ in. wide, and cut it down the centre with snips. It is well to practise with narrow hoop-iron or strips of sheet

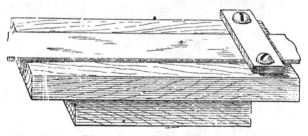

Fig. 242.—Clamp for Polishing Strip Metal.

tin before attempting a sconce in brass ; some idea of working will then be acquired on less costly material. Straighten the strips of metal on a smooth surface (as a flat-iron), using a mallet for the purpose, fix it in the vice between two boards, true the edges with flat, smooth files, and polish with emery cloth, Nos. F and O. The cloth is generally

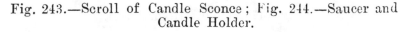

Fig. 243   Fig. 244

Fig. 243.—Scroll of Candle Sconce ; Fig. 244.—Saucer and Candle Holder.

wrapped round a flat piece of wood, $1\frac{1}{2}$ in. wide, $\frac{3}{8}$ in. thick, and 10 in. long. The flats of the strips are polished on a board (Fig. 242) about 1 ft. long, held in the vice. They should not require filing if care-

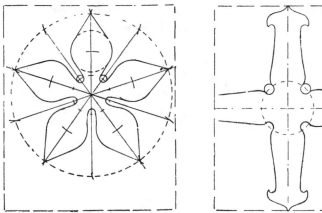

Fig. 245.—Rosette.   Fig. 246.—Candle Holder.

fully cut and straightened, but doubtful places may be draw-filed previous to polishing with emery, using Nos. 1, F, and O.

Fig. 243 gives the shape of the scroll concealed

J

by the rosettes, the small bolt passing through its
eye.   Sconces made as in Fig. 239 to swivel should be
fitted with a stop to the pivot to limit the arc of
movement.   The method of fixing the stop may be

Fig. 247.---Candle Holder Bent.

seen in the top of a gas bracket.   The scrolls are
drilled and fixed with copper rivets, and the saucer
and candle-holder are bolted on, as shown at the
section in Fig. 244, where the dotted lines represent
a winged nut.

Mark off with dividers the rosettes on thin sheet
metal (see Fig. 245), and drill small holes at the

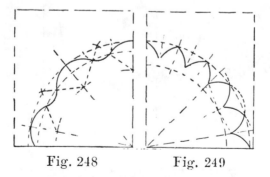

Fig. 248   Fig. 249

Figs. 248 and 249.—Candle Sconce Saucers.

division of the petals to facilitate the cutting out.
The candle-holder (Fig. 246) is treated in a similar
manner.   Two rosettes are required for Fig. 238, and
four for Fig. 239 ; they are slightly repousséd.   The

method of bending the candle-holder is shown in Fig. 247. In the vice, grip a piece of round iron with

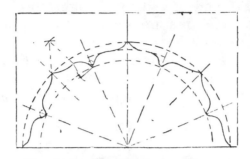

Fig. 250.—Candle Sconce Saucer.

its top end chamfered, place the metal (Fig. 246) centrally on it, and knock the petals down with a mallet. Three patterns for the edges of the saucers and

Fig. 251.—Brass or Copper Fire-screen.

methods of marking them out are shown in Figs. 248 to 250.

Figs. 251 and 252 show designs for fire-screens into which pictures on glass may be introduced. Fire-screens may have a glass painting of flowers, landscape, etc. The design shown in Fig. 251 may be made either in brass or copper, and can be constructed by an ordinary mechanic. The size of the

Fig. 252.—Wrought-iron Fire-screen.

screen will vary according to taste, or according to the size of the painted glass or plate. The feet (Fig. 253) should be of cast brass or copper, a pattern being made in wood, and then cast. The side standards are of brass or copper tubing, say $\frac{5}{8}$ in. in diameter, having cast caps and bases, into which the tube fits. These caps and bases, as shown in Fig. 254, have solid bottoms, thick enough to take a screwed pin, which for the bottom must be of square section in the centre to fit into a square hole to prevent the leg turning round. The top one on which the knob screws may be a screw pin only, The two standards thus made are fastened together

Fig. 253   Fig. 254

Fig. 253.—Foot of Fire-screen ; Fig. 254.—Cap and Base.

by two flat brass bars or tubes. A turned brass central pillar is screwed to the top brass bar, and scrolls are made in brass strip, $\frac{1}{2}$ in. by $\frac{3}{16}$ in. thick, and secured by round-headed screws to the top bar, and by a ring knob to the centre turned pillar. This ornament may be varied in several ways to suit the taste of the maker. The frame to hold the glass or picture is constructed of angle brass, soldered at the corners, and fastened to the frame with screws. The glass or picture is secured in this frame by a strip of

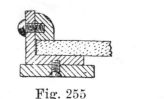

Fig. 255   Fig. 256

Figs. 255 and 256.—Fixing Glass in Fire-screen Frame.

wood fixed to it with screws, as shown in Fig. 255. The outer edge of the frame may be cut into scallop pattern, or left plain if preferred. After being fitted, the brass or copper frame should be polished and lacquered or bronzed.

Fig. 252 shows a fire-screen constructed of wrought-iron. This form could be made by anyone skilled in working in wrought-iron. The frame is made of $\frac{7}{8}$-in. angle-iron, brazed at the corners, and fitted with a wood strip, fixed with screws to hold the glass in place, as shown at Fig. 256. The legs are of flat iron, 1 in. by $\frac{3}{16}$ in., and are fixed to the under

Fig. 257

Fig. 258

Figs. 257 and 258.—Elevation and Plan of Tray Inkstand.

side of the frame with screw pins. The ornamental scrolls at the sides of the frame and at the top are made of iron, $\frac{1}{2}$ in. by $\frac{3}{16}$ in. thick, riveted together, and fastened to the iron frame with round-headed screws. The ornamental piece in the top may have a running scroll pattern, if preferred to the rings shown. When completed, the frame may be enamelled any colour to taste, or dead black.

The combined inkstand and tray shown in Fig. 257 and 258 forms a fitting companion to one of the table lamps mounted in bent iron (see pp. 101 to 103). The five main frames are made of thin

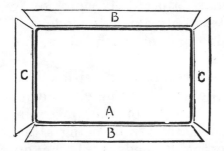

Fig. 259.—Frames of Tray Inkstand.

strips, bound together and to the scrolls; there is practically no weight upon them, so that stout iron need not be used. The frames are made by bending the thin strips to the proper angle, which is not important so long as the angles of all are alike. Fig. 259 shows the bottom frame A, the side frames B B, and the end frames C C, separated and laid down flat. The union of each frame can be made either at one corner or about the centre, by riveting, brazing, or soldering. In Figs. 260 and 261 one corner of the frames is shown enlarged and slightly

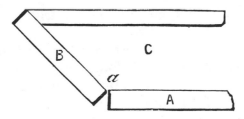

Fig. 260.—Jointing Frames of Tray Inkstand.

separated to more clearly illustrate the method of union. The frames do not come into contact throughout the whole width of the iron strips, but only at the sharp corners *a*. To make them meet, the strips would have to be set to a bevel, which

would be a troublesome job ; and more than that,
the curves that are fitted within the side and end
frames B and C would have to be set to a corresponding bevel. The binding together of the frames and
curves will make a perfectly rigid job, even though
there is contact only along the edges. The frames
are fastened together with clips, as shown in
section by Fig. 262.

The frames are filled up with curves as shown
in Fig. 258, the curves being clipped together. All
round the top edges of the outer frames scroll-
work is fastened, the scrolls being attached to each
other and to the top edges of the outer frames.

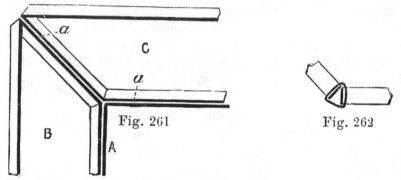

Fig. 261   Fig. 262

Fig. 261.—Jointing Frames of Tray Inkstand ; Fig. 262—
Clip at Corner of Frames.

At each of the four corners is an iron or copper
flower.

The inkpot is supported upon four series of
scroll-work set at a right angle with each other.
A series with the component curves slightly
separated is shown by Fig. 263.   Upon the top
horizontal portion of the main curve A is supported
the inkpot, the upward curve A preventing the
inkpot from sliding off sideways. This main curve
is too weak in itself to carry a large pot of ink
without yielding ; so, both for support and ornament,
minor curves are fastened to it and to each other.
The large curve B is clipped to A in three places,

a b c, but the clip *b* is not put on yet. The next curve, C, is fastened to B at *b c*. The next curve, D, is fastened to C at *f b g*. At this stage a clip is fastened round A B C D at *b*. Then curve E is fastened to B at *h j*, and to D at *k l*. Finally, the curves F G are fastened respectively to A and B at *m n* and at *o p*. The four series of curves are now fastened together at right angles with two stout clips at *q r* around a central square rod. Then the

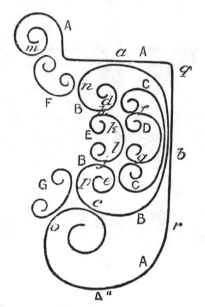

Fig. 263.—Scrollwork of Inkstand.

portion A″ of the curve A is wired or soldered to the bottom curves of the tray.

A letter rack is illustrated by Fig. 264. It may be from 6 in. to 8 in. long; but if for holding newspapers, etc., it should be made from 12 in. to 14 in. long, suspended from the wall by the eye A. If made in the small size, the framing B is of thin strips $\frac{1}{4}$ in. or $\frac{5}{16}$ in. wide. If it is of the large size, the framing should be of stout iron, $1\frac{1}{16}$ in. thick by $\frac{3}{8}$ in. wide. The framing B is a small rectangle with scarfed and brazed joints; if these are too difficult,

have plain lapped and riveted joints. Be careful
to have the iron straight and the frame free from
winding. The cross-bars c c should be fastened by
bending their ends at right angles, and then riveting or clamping them to B. The scroll work is very
simple. The S curves form a panelling, and are
clipped together and to the frames (see Fig. 264).
The scroll iron should be the same width as the
framing. The eye A at the top is formed of thin

Fig. 264.—Letter Rack.

iron, bent underneath, and soldered to the top bar
of the frame B.

The wall bracket (Figs. 265 to 267) is made en-
tirely of thin bent iron, excepting the strip A. Its
parts are the top B, the back C, and the central
supporting bracket D. The top is formed of a back
strip A of thin iron, hammered round, as shown in
detail by Figs. 268 and 269, to form a narrow bottom
flange A, which is as wide as the strips for use on
the bracket—say ⅜ in. Two slot holes b b, Fig.
266, are drilled for hanging the bracket. A stout

iron strip c is bent into a semicircle and attached to the back strip A, as shown by Figs. 268 and 269, by turning the ends of c inwards and soldering them to A. The space included between A and c is filled in with thin iron scroll-work $\frac{3}{8}$ in. or $\frac{5}{16}$ in. wide. There are four similar sets of scrolls clipped at all points

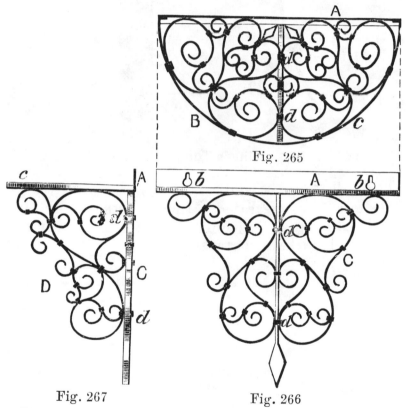

Fig. 265

Fig. 267   Fig. 266

Figs. 265 to 267.—Plan and Elevations of Wall Bracket.

of contact to each other and to the outer curve c. The back, C, of the bracket consists of duplicated scroll work, with a central arrow point or finial. The curves are united for the most part with clips, but at the top, where they come in contact with the narrow flange of the back, A, clips cannot be used because the back is of solid sheet, and they must here be soldered. The supporting bracket D is clipped to the back and to the top curves at the points *d d.* These clips are all illus-

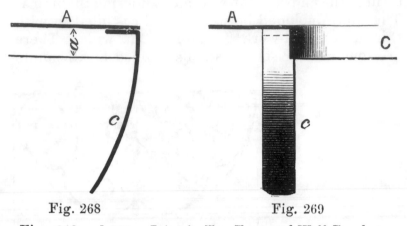

Fig. 268   Fig. 269

Figs. 268 and 269.—Joint in Top Frame of Wall Bracket.

trated in Figs. 266 and 267, but necessarily their thickness is exaggerated. In the actual work, if done neatly, the clips add very little to the thickness of the parts in contact.

INDEX.

Acid Bath for Brass, 19, 64
Annealing Iron, 118
Anvil, 14

Ball Bolts, 59
Balls, Bent Iron, 70, 71
——, Sheet Metal, 124
Bedroom Candlestick, 56—58
Bench Anvil, 14
—— Hammer, 13
—— Stake, 14
—— Vice, 14
Bending Hook on Iron Bar, 112
—— Iron Bar, 51, 61
—— Strip Metal into Scrolls,
    15—18, 21, 22
Bent Iron Work, Advantages of, 9
—— —— ——, Black Polishing, 18
—— —— ——, Dead Blacking, 18
Blacksmithing and Forging, 14,
    51, 52
Block, Lead, 48, 49
——, Pitch, 44, 46
——, Scroll, 15
Bolts, Ball, 59
Border, Bent Iron, 24
Bowl, Hanging Flower, 42, 43,
    112—114
——, Mount, 35—37
Bracket Candlesticks, 50—54
——, Lamp, 33—35, 110
——, Suspension, 66
——, Wall, 154—156
Brass Candle-sconces, 142
——, Dipping, 19, 64, 65
——, Lacquering, 19
——, Lacquers for, 19, 20
—— Ornaments, Repoussé, 94
—— Rosettes, 146
—— Strip, 10
—— ——, Polishing, with Emery
    Cloth, 145
Brazing, 28, 29

C Scrolls, 22
Candle-holders, 54, 56, 146, 147
Candle-sconces, 142—148
Candlesticks, Bedroom, 56—58
——, Bracket, 50—54
——, Reading-table, 54—58
Cathedral Grilles, 84—92
Chains, Suspension, 24, 107, 109
——, ——, Twisting, 120
Chichester Cathedral, Grille at,
    87, 88
Cinquefoil Cluster, 87
Clamp for Strip Metal, 145
Clipping Glass in Position, 73, 83
Clips, 13, 22
Colouring Copper, 97, 98
Concave Hammering, 49
—— Punching, 44, 46
Copper, Colouring, 97, 98
—— Flowers, 44—48
——, Lacquering, 19
—— Leaves, 48
—— Rosettes, 118
—— Strip, 10
—— Trefoils, 48, 49
Corner Joints, 78
Cup-head Rivets, 29
Curves, Bending, 15—18, 21, 22
——, Forms of, 21—24
Cutting Pliers, 11, 12

Dipping Brass, 64, 65
Drilling Holes in Strips, 31
Dumping-up Iron Bar, 51

Ecclesiastical Grilles and
    Screens, 84—92
Emery Cloth, Polishing Brass
    Strip with, 145
Eleanor Grille at Westminster
    Abbey, 88—90

Fern Vessel, Suspended, 112—114

Fire-guard, 92—95
Fire-screens, 78—84, 92—100
—— with Pictures, 148—150
Flat-nosed Pliers, 12, 13
Floor Lamp, 131—141
Floral Ornaments, 44—49
—— ——: Leaves, 22, 24, 48, 104, 124
—— ——: Rosettes 56, 82, 118, 146
Florence, Santa Croce, Grille at, 90, 91
Flower Vase or Bowl, Hanging, 42, 43, 112—114
Flowers, Copper, 44—48
Forge Work, 51, 52
Fork for Bending Scrolls, 16
Frames, Double Photograph, 121, 126, 127
——, Single Photograph, 123—126
Framings of Bent Iron Work, 24, 25
——, Brazing, 28, 29
——, Riveting, 29—32
——, Soft Soldering, 26, 28
Freiburg Cathedral, Grille at, 91

Gas Lamps, Hall, 115—120
Glass Bowl Mount, 35—37
—— ——, Suspended, 42, 43, 112—114
——, Clipping, in Position, 73
——, Securing, 83, 84
Gloves worn at Work, 14
Grille at Chichester Cathedral, 37, 88
—— —— Florence, 90, 91
—— —— Freiburg Cathedral, 91
—— —— Lincoln Cathedral, 87
—— —— Puy-en-Velay, 87
—— —— St. Denis, 90
—— —— Santa Croce, 90, 91
—— —— Westminster Abbey, 88—90
—— —— Winchester Cathedral, 85—87
——, Eleanor, 88—90
Grilles, 84—100
Guard, Fire, 92—95

Hall Lamps, 107—110, 115—120
—— Lantern Brackets, 66
—— —— Hanger, 66

Hall Lanterns, 59—77
Hammer, 13
Hammering Hollow or Concave, 49
Hanging Flower Vase or Bowl, 42, 43, 112—114
—— Lamps, 107—110, 115, 120
—— Lanterns, 59—77
Heart Scroll, 22
Hollowing with Hammer, 49
—— —— Punch, 44, 46
Hook, Forming, on Iron Bar, 112

Incandescent Gas Lamps, Hall, 115—120
Inkpot, Mount for, 152
Inkstand combined with Tray, 151
Invalids, Bent Iron Work suitable for, 9
Iron, Annealing, 118
—— Bar, Bending, 51, 61
—— ——, Forming Hook on, 112
—— ——, Upsetting, 51
—— ——, Welding, 52
—— Strip, 9, 10

Joints, Brazed,
——, Corner Riveted, 78
——, Cross Riveted, 78
——, Lapped, 78
——, Riveted, 31, 32
——, Scarfed, 64, 78
——, Seam, 40
——, Soldered, 26, 28
——, Sweated, 26, 28
——, Wired, 36

Killed Spirits of Salts, 26

Lacquering Brass, Copper, and Tin, 19, 20
Lacquers, Recipes for, 19, 20
Ladies, Bent Iron Work suitable for, 9
——, Gloves to be worn by, 14
Lamp Bracket, 33—35, 110
——, Floor, 131—141
——, ——, Telescopic Arrangement of, 136
——, Hanging, 107—110, 115—120
—— Shades, 136

Lamp, Standard, 131—141
——, ——, Telescopic Arrangement of, 136
——, Suspended, 107—110, 115—120
——, Table, 101—106
—— Tray, Hall Lantern, 63
——, Wall, 110
Lantern Brackets, 66
—— Hanger, 66
Lanterns, Hall, 59—77
Lapped Joint, 78
Lead Block, 48, 49
Letter Rack, 128—130, 153, 154
Leaves, Bent Iron, 22, 24
——, Sheet Metal, 48, 94, 104, 124
Lincoln Cathedral, Grille at, 87

Magazine Rack, 128—130. 153, 154
Mandrels, Bending Strips round, 18
Materials and Tools, 9—20
Moulds for Making Scrolls, 15
Mounts, Glass Bowl, 35—37
——, Inkpot, 152
——, Table Lamp, 101—106
——, Vase, 37—42

Newspaper, Rack, 128—130, 153, 154

Ornaments, Floral, 44—49
——, Leaf, 22, 24, 48, 94, 104, 124
——, Repoussé Brass, 94
——, Rosette, 56, 82, 118, 146

Panels, 130
Paper Rack, 128—130, 153, 154
Petals of Copper Flowers, 44—48
Photograph Frame, Double, 121, 126, 127
—— ——, Single, 123—126
Pincers, 13
Pins for Bending Scrolls, 18
Pitch Block, 44, 46
Pliers, Cutting, 11, 12
——, Flat-nosed, 12, 13
——, Round-nosed, 12
Polishing Brass Strips, 145
—— —— ——, Clamp for, 145
Punches, 13, 29
Punching Copper Flowers, 44, 46
—— Holes in Strips, 13, 29—31

Punching, Hollow or Concave, 44, 46
Puy-en-Velay, Grille at, 87

Quatrefoil, 51
—— Panels of Grille, 90

Rack, Newspaper, etc., 128—130, 153, 154
Reading-table, Candlestick for, 54—56
Reamer, 13
Repoussé Brass Ornament, 94
—— Screen, 97, 99
Ribbon Metal, 9, 10
Riveting, 31, 32, 78
Rivets, Cup-head, 29
——, Drilling Holes for, 29, 31
——, Flat-head, 29
——, Punching Holes for 13, 29—31
——, Sizes of, 29
——, Snap, 29
Rosettes, 56, 82, 118, 146
Round-nosed Pliers, 12

S Scrolls, 22, 24
St. Denis, Grille at, 90
Santa Croce, Grille at, 90, 91
Scarfed Joint, 64, 78
Sconces, Candle, 142—148
Screens, 78—100
——, Fire, 78—84, 92—100
Scrolls, Ascertaining Length of, 117, 144
——, Bending, 15—18, 21, 22
——, Blocks and Moulds for, 15
——, C, 22
——, Fork for Bending, 16
——, Forms of, 21—24
——, Heart, 22
——, Pins for Bending, 18
——, S, 22, 24
——, Wrench for Bending, 16—18
——, Wrought-iron, 15
Seam Joint, 40
Shades, Lamp, 136
Smiths' Work, 14, 51, 52
Snap, 32
—— Rivets, 29
Snips, Tinmen's, 10
Soldering with Copper-bit, 26
—— Fluid, 26

Soldering, Hard, 23
—— by Sweating-on, 26, 28
Spirits, Killed, 26
Stake, Bench, 14
Stamens of Copper Flowers, 44—48
Standard Lamp, 131—141
Star Designs, 69, 70, 107, 109, 113
Strip Brass, 10
—— ——, Clamp for, 145
—— ——, Polishing, with Emery Cloth, 145
—— Metal, 9, 10
Suspended Flower Vases and Bowls, 42, 43, 112—114
—— Lamps, 107—110, 115—120
—— Lanterns, 59—77
Suspension Brackets, 66
—— Chains, 24, 107, 109
—— ——, Twisting 120
Sweating-on Process of Soldering, 26, 28

Table Candlesticks, 54—58
—— Lamps, 101—106
Telescopic Arrangement of Floor Lamp, 136
Tendrils, Bent Iron, 24
Tin, Lacquering, 20
——, Lacquers for, 20
Tinmen's Snips, 10

Tin-plate Strip, 10
Tools for Bent Iron Work, 10—20
Tray combined with Inkstand, 151
——, Lamp, of Hall Lantern, 63
Trefoils, Copper, 48, 49
Twist Ornament, 24, 120

Upsetting Iron Bar, 51

Vase Mounts, 37—42
Vases, Suspended Flower, 42, 43, 112—114
Vice, 14
Volute Curves, 21—24 (see also Scrolls)

Wall Bracket, 154—156
—— Lamp, 110
Welding Iron, 52
Westminster Abbey, Grille at, 88—90
Winchester Cathedral, Grille at, 85—87
Wire Shades for Lamps, 136
Wired Joint, 36`
Wrench for Bending Scrolls, 16—18
Wrought-iron Leaves, etc., 94
—— Scrolls, 15

Zigzag Pattern, 76

PRINTED BY CASSELL & COMPANY, LIMITED, LUDGATE HILL, LONDON, E.C.